Praise for Unshattered Dreams

"Using the combination of skills as a life coach, therapist, and motivational interviewing, Paul Novello has written a fine book. Daring to share his personal life growing up and demonstrating vulnerability allows the reader to do the same. Paul writes: 'One of my intentions in writing this book has been to take the pain of what my family and I experienced and use it as a platform to empower and inspire you.' Paul has done this and so much more in writing this book."

> —Joe Kort, Ph.D., author of *10 Smart Things Gay Men Can Do to Improve Their Lives*

"In this compelling and inspiring book, Paul guides us on a journey of personal transformation. By combining his insight and skills as a professional therapist and life coach with his personal experience of overcoming a difficult childhood, Paul demonstrates the courage needed to change. Paul's honesty gives all of us hope to do the same."

> —Rich German, author of *Monetize Your Passion*

"Much of what Paul shares in this fantastic, saddening, maddening, and powerful book is all too familiar in my work with children, adults, and families. Reading his history and its devastating impact in black and white makes it so much more potent than just reading it through a clinical lens. Paul has shown us how he has risen above the torments of his childhood in their various forms and created not only his own path toward success, but utilizes what he's learned as a guide for others to be successful as well. The strength and wonder of love, resilience, generosity, and compassion radiate throughout Paul's life and this book. I am honored to have a colleague and a close friend with such beauty. Thank you, Paul, for letting us into your world."

  —Ken Wilson, Psy.D., Clinical psychologist and adolescent behavioral health researcher

"Whether your childhood was horrific or just mildly dysfunctional, Paul Novello's *Unshattered Dreams* will help you understand and overcome your childhood drama to live a happier and more successful life. Combining his own experiences growing up with an abusive and alcoholic father with his knowledge as a therapist and life coach, Paul is able to offer real, actionable healing solutions. For years I was in the dark on why I wasn't able to live the life I wanted and felt I deserved. Now I understand."

  —Tom Luke, Owner of Luke Direct Marketing and
  Healthy Gay Lifestyles Magazine

Unshattered Dreams

Unshattered Dreams

An Inspirational Guide to a
Happy and Successful Life
after a Difficult Childhood

Paul Novello

Life Solutions Publishing
New York, N.Y.

Publisher: Life Solutions Publishing
Email: unshattereddreams@gmail.com
Website: www.unshattereddreams.com

Editing by Stephanie Gunning
Book design by Gus Yoo

Library of Congress Control Number: 2012922392
ISBN 978-0-9882960-2-2 (paperback)
ISBN 978-0-9882960-3-9 (ebook)

1. Self-help 2. Personal transformation 3. Gay and lesbian
4. Recovery 5. Mental health 6. Substance abuse 7. Abuse
8. Success 9. Self-esteem 10. Happiness

This book is dedicated to my mother,
a constant pillar of strength
and a beacon of light

Contents

Bless the Beasts and the Children

(Words and music by Barry DeVorzon
and Perry Botkin, Jr.)

Bless the beasts and the children
For in this world they have no voice
They have no choice

Bless the beasts and the children
For the world can never be
The world they see

Light their way
When the darkness surrounds them
Give them love
Let it shine all around them

Bless the beasts and the children
Give them shelter from the storm
Keep them safe
Keep them warm

Preface

"All glory comes from daring to begin."
—Eugene F. Ware

Congratulations. By picking up this book you have taken the first step on your journey to wholeness. If you had a difficult childhood, you know that there are many challenges you are still struggling with in your life. These "ghosts" from the past may continue to haunt you today, but you hold the power to chase them away. You have the power of choice. You can choose to change your thoughts and take positive actions to heal yourself from the emotional and psychological wounds of the past, or you can remain stuck in blame and negativity over why your life hasn't turned out the way you wanted.

This book will help you realize how your childhood has affected your adult life. Whether you are having relationship, health, or career challenges, financial difficulties, interpersonal conflicts, or problems with addiction, the way that you respond to these events depends on who you are today. As a child from an abusive or neglectful home, the coping skills you developed to survive may no longer serve you.

This book will show you the specific steps you can take to make positive changes in your life . . . today. Consider it a roadmap to guide you on your path. If you embrace the information and take the steps I am offering you here, I guarantee that your life will change for the better. You will begin to grow, prosper, and flourish, and your life will unfold in ways you have never dreamed were possible.

This book is not an in-depth psychological study, nor does it explore the different therapeutic techniques that may be available to you to treat your specific problems. I am writing from my own experience of growing up in a dysfunctional family with a violent, alcoholic father, and from my professional perspective as a therapist and life coach. Additionally, this book is not meant to replace any type of counseling or psychotherapy that you may require, although you can certainly use the concepts as an auxiliary to any professional treatment you may receive. At the end of the book I have included a list of resources to help get you started on your healing path if you have not done so already. Every chapter also includes specific growth tips that summarize the particular action steps you can take to move forward.

I wish you great success on your journey.

Introduction

"In the depth of winter, I finally learned that there was within me an invincible summer."
—Albert Camus

I wrote this book to inspire you. I want you to know that no matter how painful your life was as a child, you can find positive solutions to heal your wounds, release the past, and live a happy and successful life. I can tell you this with absolute certainty because I am living proof that it is possible. I was raised by an abusive, alcoholic father who inflicted routine acts of violence upon my family. As a child, I struggled with countless disappointments and losses. I lived in constant chaos, fear, and uncertainty because I never knew what type of situations I would encounter on any given day. Due to the negative effects of my childhood, I ultimately had to build my life, not from zero, but from below that neutral point, just to begin to be on equal ground with others.

Today, I live a very happy, successful, and rewarding life. I am blessed with glowing health, loving and harmonious relationships, and tremendous satisfaction in my work and career. I am financially successful, even having built all of my financial resources from nothing. In part, this book is based on my life story and experiences. My intention is to speak to you as honestly and openly as I would a trusted friend. Therefore, I will highlight some of the personal challenges I faced along the way for illustration.

My intention in writing this book is to educate, inspire, and empower you on your own personal journey of healing so that you, too, can release the bondage of a difficult childhood and transition to being a happy and successful adult. It doesn't matter what age you are when you begin because growth is a never-ending and evolving process. So whether you are an adolescent just getting started or an adult who "knows it all," in reading this book you will gain valuable insights and practical skills that will put your childhood into perspective, help you take control, and improve the quality of your life. With increased awareness and greater understanding you can implement the necessary strategies to change your life for the better and improve your current view of the world.

Everyone has memories and perceptions of childhood experiences that hurt them. Some adults had horrible childhoods. Others had average upbringings. A few fortunate ones had a wonderful time growing up. Despite these differences, we all share similar feelings of being mistreated or slighted by others. However, some "perceived" forms of mistreatment might not really be mistreatment at all. Perhaps a person felt unjustly treated because a sibling received more attention, time, or love from a parent than he or she did. This may have merely been sibling rivalry or jealousy without any actual abuse or neglect whatsoever. But to the person who experienced this, it is a very real emotional and psychological pain. Furthermore, if this was a consistent pattern within the family, and the parents showed favoritism to one child over another, it could certainly interfere with the person's success and enjoyment of life as an adult. This is especially true if the person dwells on the situation, harbor resentments, and continues to allow this past dynamic to exert power over him or her.

Not all childhood "mistreatment" is obvious and clear. Some is more subtle and covert, but every experience is real and valid to the person who lived through it.

Abused and neglected children can develop severe psychological and emotional problems, including low self-esteem, fear, anger, stress, anxiety, depression, guilt, and shame. They may also have social and relationship difficulties, addictions, and financial and health problems that can follow them way into adulthood. I'll explore these issues more fully later on.

As adolescents and adults try to cope with oppressive issues of the past, they often have difficulty adjusting to life in the present. Dealing with the stress of everyday living can be overwhelming for anyone, but for survivors of abuse it can also cause the shadows of past hurts and traumas to resurface. This can be immobilizing for someone trying to handle a present conflict while also being burdened with the past. Clearly, this is problematic for the individual; it often is tough for the people around him or her, too.

Conversely, some people who survive childhood abuse become steadfast overachievers. Like super heroes, they take on whatever comes their way. They are always trying to please others, while often neglecting themselves. These are action-oriented people who have trouble setting limits and saying no, a tendency that can lead to increased stress and has a high potential for burnout.

On the positive side, however, children from tough backgrounds are tried, tested, and challenged in unusual ways. They have learned how to cope under extremely dire circumstances. These children have wonderful qualities and strengths that can serve them well into adulthood. They can be resilient, determined, and creative, and often have a high tolerance for dealing with difficult situations that could easily throw others into a complete tailspin.

After surviving the aftermath of such troubling childhood circumstances, many people are left feeling shocked, traumatized, and confused. They seem lost, often wondering, *Where do I go from here?* These adolescents or adults now have to figure out how to pick up the shattered pieces of their lives and be happy, healthy, and successful. Unfortunately, many of them never do. Like their parents, they tend to develop their own self-destructive ways because this is what is familiar.

The purpose of this book is to help you recognize the pitfalls of emerging from a difficult childhood and discover how to rise above them. You will become increasingly self-aware, and learn to drop your excuses and be accountable for the thoughts you think, the decisions you make, and the actions you take. Taking 100 percent responsibility for your behavior and well-being will lead you to live a happier, and more fulfilled and successful life.

My hope is that you embrace the information in this book and use it to heal and improve your life. I want you to reach for the unshattered dreams that are still alive within you. Your unshattered dreams are the parts of you that remain whole and complete despite anything that happened to you. These are your strengths, talents, capabilities, your intellect, and your heart's desires. No matter what happened during your difficult childhood, no one can ever destroy your unshattered dreams. They are yours to have and to hold. You may have tucked them away deep inside of you, but trust me, they are there yearning for expression. Believe that you can rise above the past, create the life you want, and fulfill your unshattered dreams, for this is the life you were meant to live.

I've done it and so can you.

Remember, the power to change your life is always within you.

Part One

How to Recognize the Impact
of a Difficult Childhood and
What You Can Do about It

"Nothing is predestined: The obstacles of your past can become the gateways that lead to new beginnings."
—Ralph Blum

Part One of this book is designed to guide you on a journey to overcome the emotional and psychological wounds of your difficult childhood. It addresses the areas that are important for you to explore and resolve so that you can get clear to live a happy and successful life. Part One details a therapeutic approach, as the focus is on healing and recovery.

Once you have resolved the issues from your childhood, you will have gained the presence of mind to build your vision for the future so that you can create the life you truly desire.

CHAPTER ONE

"I'm Fine...Really!"

"Denial ain't just a river in Egypt."
—Mark Twain

It's not easy to examine our emotional pain, so most of us will do whatever we can to avoid it. Let's face it: Denial is nature's way of protecting us from harm. Besides, who wants to be reminded of painful experiences anyway, right?

The trouble with this is that denial keeps us from being accountable for our actions because it means we can blame others or make excuses for why things don't work rather than looking within. Denial stops us from growing, and keeps us from reaching our goals and unshattered dreams. Coming out of denial may make you feel uncomfortable or uneasy at times. This does not negate its value. Just remember, it is always darkest before the dawn. Although it might be hard for you at first, you can and will get through to the other side. If you came this far, you are a survivor. This means you have all the inner strength and resources you need, so stay focused and keep going.

It's hard to accept that your parents didn't meet your needs. Although people can generally acknowledge that they had a difficult childhood, it is not always easy for them to recognize and accept that it had an impact. Life always has a way of giving us wake-up calls though; we just have to be ready and willing to answer them. Life holds up a mirror and is always reflecting back to us what we need to know. Our life circumstances will always reveal the truth of what is going on inside of us.

As a child, I was bounced around from place to place due to my father's alcoholism. We lost our home and my parents divorced when I was twelve. My parents remained together on and off for several years after the divorce, and the family continued on a downward spiral. My father always promised to change and pleaded for my mother to take him back because he said he *didn't want to lose his family.* My mother, being the compassionate and loving person that she is, always believed him and yielded to his promises.

My brother, sister, and I were caught in a vicious cycle of leaving my father, relocating, and then having him move back in with us. When our parents' divorce occurred, we were pulled from a beautiful home on Long Island, New York, and taken to live in my aunt's basement apartment in Queens. After several weeks, my father moved back in with us. We were now five people living in a cramped three-room basement apartment.

I was always hopeful that my father would change his behavior and that things would improve. Unfortunately, his drinking and violently abusive ways always resumed. My mother unsuccessfully tried to break free time and time again. We moved at least eleven times within five years. As a result of this constant upheaval, I was enrolled into many different schools during critical years in my development. Over and over again everything familiar was stripped away from me: I lost all my childhood friends and was forced to adjust to new people and constantly changing circumstances. Consequently, I became an isolated, shy, and withdrawn kid who was discouraged and depressed.

Trying to survive the chaos and trauma at home delayed my adolescent development. I completely shut down and was not ready to deal with my sexuality. I just had too many daily challenges to face so I pushed the fact that I was gay out of my mind. I looked for ways to channel my feelings and escaped into a world of fantasy. Fortunately, I was always a very creative and artistic child with a natural talent for performing. I developed various ways to entertain myself. This was in the days before cable television, computers, video games, VCRs, and iPods. I used to love to imitate performers. I acted out various skits I watched on television and sang songs I heard on the radio. I also learned to play the piano that was kept upstairs in my aunt's house. I immersed myself in performing and knew this was my chosen path. I constantly fantasized about how different my life would be when my career as a professional performer took off, and this fantasy gave me incredible hope and optimism for the future.

In retrospect, I was fortunate to have found a positive outlet for my emotional pain, rather than slipping into alcohol, drug abuse, or other negative behaviors as so many children from dysfunctional families do. Years later, I realized that my soul had been seeking self-expression through my desire to perform. I yearned to communicate all the things I felt inside but was too afraid to express or experience at the time. I wanted to be noticed, loved, and accepted, so I focused all of my energies on becoming an actor and singer. Although this might seem stereotypical of every gay boy's fantasy, to me it was a very real desire. My ultimate dream was to act, sing, and star on Broadway.

School was another source of horror for me. After my parents split up, I was taken from the Long Island Public School System, a relatively small homogenous suburban setting, and was placed into the New York City Public

School System, a much larger urban setting where the kids were tougher and slick. Not only was I traumatized from my home life, now I also had to deal with the culture shock of living and going to school in the city, which was quite overwhelming. Since I was nervous, withdrawn, and always the new kid on the block, I became an easy target for bullying and harassment at school. This went on for several years because I never remained at the same school long enough to establish any solid friendships. I remained isolated, lonely, and retreated inward during my adolescence. Life pretty much sucked.

The only light I saw was in the field of music and acting, and in my hopes and dreams for a better life. I was once given an opportunity to unleash my talent when I was asked to do a reading from the play *All My Sons* by Arthur Miller in my high school English class. The monologue was quite emotional and touched upon the conflict between a father and son—right up my alley! Somehow I was able to summon the emotional intensity that was required for the scene and my reading blew the class away. I was able to be confident and strong through a character in a play. In that moment, I found I could assert myself and say want I wanted to say through someone else's words. In connecting with the character I felt free to do, be, and say what I couldn't in my own life. After my reading, the entire class applauded. I guess they just couldn't believe what was coming out of this shy and quiet kid. I was thrilled at the attention and recognition I received, and this reinforced my desire to be an actor.

Although I had talent, I was an insecure adolescent, which was a constant barrier for me. It wasn't until I began to study acting and singing and perform in the theatre that I realized I had some real problems, however. Each time I went on stage or in front of class I became nervous until I started to perform. My nerves usually subsided once I got into the character and the life of the play. My teachers constantly told me to relax, but I didn't know how. Frankly, I didn't even know what they meant. I lacked self-awareness and struggled with low self-esteem. I took criticism personally and always worked that much harder to improve and prove myself. No one had a clue about what I was going through or that I was carrying around a lot of past and present trauma. I never said anything to anyone about my home life.

I was in deep denial for a long time that my childhood experiences had any effect on me whatsoever, because to me my life was normal. I honestly believe that my desire to perform saved me. As I continued to study, it forced me to look at myself. Eventually I opened up to one of my closest teachers and revealed what was going on at home. My teacher provided much needed empathy, as she validated and understood what I was going through. She also helped me to connect my current tension and anxiety to my upbringing, and suggested that I consider attending Al-Anon meetings and get some counseling. With my teacher's ongoing support, the insights I gained, and my willingness to grow and change, I began my journey on the road to self-discovery.

I share all this with you to say that self-awareness is the key that unlocks the door. Once you recognize and accept that you have a problem you can do something about it. Until then, for as long as the denial lasts, you'll be stuck.

Although denial is a self-protective mechanism, it can be a double-edged sword. Some denial is helpful because it gives you time to grasp certain traumatic experiences or stressful events. But by staying in the denial phase too long you keep yourself from being able to take action. Most denial is unconscious, however, if someone you trust continues to tell you that you might be in denial or if you remain stuck by repeating the same experiences over and over again, try to take an honest look at yourself. This means you are becoming consciously aware of ingrained patterns. Once you acknowledge them, you can start to change.

Seek support from a trusted friend or family member. Find a good therapist or support group. Do research to learn about the issues you are struggling with. Once I began to recognize the impact of my difficult childhood and moved out of denial an entirely new world opened up to me. I discovered that there was a whole recovery movement of which I could be a part. I learned about growing up in an alcoholic family and the various roles family members take on to compensate for the dysfunction. I found out about support groups, such as Adult Children of Alcoholics (ACOA) and Al-Anon for family members of alcoholics. I no longer felt so alone.

In addition, I located a therapist and underwent counseling. I developed an appetite for reading self-help books to educate myself. Most importantly, I was open and receptive to growth and change, which is crucial to recovery. Allow yourself to be like a sponge and absorb as much insight and information as possible. In doing so, you will identify with what you learn. You will feel validated, supported, and connected as you heal, and this is extremely comforting.

GROWTH TIPS

Self-awareness is the key to unlocking denial. Open the door to acceptance and ask for help. Seek assistance and counsel from trusted resources (friends, family members, therapists, support groups, or clergy members). Talk about your experiences to get validation and support. Join a support group in your local area. Research, read, and educate yourself about the issues that are most troubling to you. Congratulate yourself for having the courage to examine your life as it was and as it is today. Know that you can make positive changes to create the life you truly want.

CHAPTER TWO

"What's My Problem?"

*"The more anger towards the past you carry
in your heart, the less capable you are
of loving in the present."*
—Barbara De Angelis

C hildhood is expected to be a time of great joy.
Children are supposed to be nurtured, loved, and
taught all the things they need to know to succeed
in the world. Children should be encouraged to explore
their unique talents and capabilities in a loving environment that fosters growth and security.

At the beginning of life, children are naturally curious

about everything. Their young minds are open to new information, as they absorb everything around them with all of their senses. Research shows that babies start to experience life even before they are born. They hear sounds and voices *in utero* to which they grow accustomed. Their early learning experiences come directly from within the family. Babies quickly learn how to influence the people around them. They recognize that certain cries bring food, comfort, and love.

A child's fastest rate of learning occurs between birth and age three, with rapid learning that continues to age five. Naturally, parents have the most influence on a child's learning during this crucial time. Some of the most important aspects of learning are in the areas of communication, cognition, physical development, and mobility, self-esteem, problem solving, creativity, and learning how to relate to their social environment. Children learn and develop more of these skills when they are raised in a nurturing, loving, and secure environment.

In order to boost a child's sense of confidence, self-esteem, and positive social development, parents must provide the following:

- A loving, safe, and supportive environment.
- Encouragement to explore and try new things.
- Praise for accomplishments and for attempts to accomplish tasks.
- Dedicated and focused quality time that demon-

strates interest, care, and enjoyment of the time spent together.
- The ability to learn and build on existing strengths and skills and to develop new ones.
- Positive words, feedback, and support.
- Empathy and concern when the child needs to talk or express his or her fears and concerns.
- Verbalization that helps the child express how he or she feels about certain situations.
- Guidance on how to get along with adults and other children, and how to handle different social situations/interactions.
- Education and information to help the child better understand people, his or her environment, and the world.
- Opportunities for the child to learn by doing tasks that will allow him or her to succeed without failure, fear, or negative criticism.
- Toys, objects, and activities that the child is interested in exploring, and that bring him or her pleasure.
- Time to laugh, be silly, and have fun.
- Opportunities for the child to interact with other children and adults apart from his or her own parents.

Parents who provide supportive teaching and activities to their children allow them to gain valuable skills in their formative years, thereby giving them a lasting foundation throughout their lives. A childhood filled with fond memories of nurturing, loving, and supportive parents who offer ample opportunities to develop emotionally and psychologically prepares them for adulthood. These children develop positive self-esteem, confidence, and a healthy self-image that will help them to face the world.

Children who are abused or neglected start to build emotional walls and self-defense mechanisms to protect themselves. Their parents' treatment of them causes them to develop feelings of anger, resentment, and even hatred toward their parents instead of the healthy minds, emotions, and skills previously mentioned.

Identifying the Difficult Childhood

Almost everyone has some gripes about his or her childhood. If asked, many people will say that they had a "difficult childhood." Consider this, though, in light of people who suffered through years of abuse or neglect. Many of these individuals were on the receiving end of physical, verbal, and emotional abuse. Some experienced frigid detachment and heart-breaking cruelty. These are the people who experienced truly difficult childhoods. The number of those who grew up under horrible conditions only represents a fraction of those who self-identify as having led a difficult childhood.

Of course, this does not mean that those who have complaints or unresolved childhood issues should have their concerns disregarded because they did not experience serious trauma. There is a distinction, however, between those who had flawed childhoods and those who had truly difficult childhoods. It is a matter of the level of severity.

It's important for you to recognize this distinction when assessing your own history. Understanding the true nature of your background and the difficulty that you endured is an important part of making progress. Clearly, different backgrounds require different interventions and treatment approaches. If you lived through a relatively normal, but somewhat problematic childhood, you may just have some minor issues to resolve. On the other hand, if you are carrying around physical or emotional scars from a truly difficult background, your needs will be much more intense.

Obviously, those who had "less than perfect" upbringings won't benefit from following the treatment protocols for those who suffered unjustly in their formative years. Those experiences and needs are way too different.

As one of three children, I witnessed numerous acts of violence inflicted upon my family by my father. Most of these events were directed at my older brother, who was the primary target for my father's rage and aggression. As a young boy I watched my brother constantly tormented and abused. I saw him chased with shovels, knives, and other blunt objects. My father once aimed a real bow and arrow at my brother, making him run to avoid getting hit.

At the age of ten, my brother joined the Cub Scouts. My parents planned to take him to his first meeting, and my brother was dressed in his new uniform eagerly waiting to go. My father got drunk and refused to go to the meeting. Not to disappoint my brother, my mother told him that she would take him there herself. When my drunken father heard this, he started a fight with my mother to prevent them from going. He became so enraged that he took the kitchen garbage and threw it all over the kitchen and at my brother in his brand-new Cub Scout uniform. My brother cried, "It's okay, Mommy . . . we don't have to go," as garbage dripped and fell all over him.

Throughout the years, my mother constantly acted as a referee, to protect the life of her oldest son and other children. She frequently had to insert herself between my father and brother to prevent my brother from getting hurt. As the youngest child, I was always terrified and angry because I was too powerless to help. I lived in constant fear that my father's rage and aggression would ultimately be directed at me. I reacted by hiding and withdrawing to avoid him. I always tried to be a perfect kid so that nothing would ever happen to me. I lived with knots in my stomach and frequently trembled in my bed at night in anticipation of the next tirade.

As children, me and my siblings were raised in a war zone. We never knew what we would encounter when we came home from school or from a visit to friend's house. On one occasion, I came home to find my father in a drunken rage busting up all of the dining room furniture. Each chair was taken, smashed over the table, and destroyed. The legs of the table were broken off and flung across the room. There was broken wood and furniture all over the house. He went further and grabbed food out of the refrigerator, throwing it against the walls, and afterwards smashed the inside shelves of the refrigerator door. There were all types of foods mixed with spaghetti and sauce running down the kitchen walls. This was only one of a countless number of events like this. My father was always destructive when he was in a drunken angry state.

There were many "night raids," as I call them. My father would come home from binge drinking during the early morning hours and instigate a fight with my mother. She generally tried to ignore him to keep peace in the house, so he would get aggravated and start in on us kids. At one or two in the morning he would bang on our bedroom doors while we were asleep, fling them open, and scream, "Get the fuck up, you motherfuckers! I'm up . . . everybody's up!" He would then flick on the lights, pull the covers off of my brother, and the horror would begin. My brother and I shared the same bedroom so I always woke up to this nightmare.

My father's physical and verbal harassment, and screaming would continue into the early morning hours, and we frequently missed school the next day. The police were usually called to the house. At times they would take my father away, which provided a momentary sigh of relief and sense of security, but they never kept him for too long. Things were quite different in the 1970s. Today, this would be considered a domestic violence situation and it would be handled much differently.

Following these episodes, my father would sober up and get quiet and meek. He was plagued with the "shakes" and anxiety attacks due to alcohol withdrawal. His crying and whimpering usually scared me as much as his drunkenness.

I have vivid memories of events that had direct hits on me as well. When I was five, my mother promised to take me to see the movie *Chitty Chitty Bang Bang.* We planned to go one Saturday afternoon, but my drunken father wouldn't let us. He fought with my mother and disconnected the wires on the car so she couldn't take me. I started to cry, but my incredible mother refused to break her promise to me. She defied my father, called a taxi, and took me to see the movie. We had a great afternoon, just the two of us. I loved the film and will never forget what my mother did for me that day. This was not unusual, however, because my mother was always there for me. She was the only one I could ever rely on. She was both mother and father to me.

My mother's actions had a profound effect on me growing up, and I am very fortunate to have had her positive influence. Many children are not so lucky. My mother demonstrated incredible strength and personal power throughout the years and I unconsciously learned to rely on my own inner strength and power as well by watching her example. Christmas was and still is my favorite holiday. Mom always made it special for us. Despite some of the tragic holidays we had while growing up, I always cherished the holiday season and looked upon it with great hope and joy. I also developed a passion for design and love to decorate . . . (yes, I got that "gay gene," too).

I had a friend whose father always put up the most elaborate display of Christmas lights on the block. One year I was at my friend's house watching him and his father bond as they created incredible scenes with lights and decorations. I was very excited and inspired and ran home to ask my father to do the same. He was drinking again and refused to put up the Christmas decorations. I begged and pleaded, but he just got increasingly agitated and angry. I knew all too well what would follow and so I stopped asking.

Angry and disappointed, I took matters into my own hands. I went down to the basement storage room, found a strand of lights, and decided to decorate myself. These were the old-fashioned lights with the big screw in light bulbs and they weren't so easy to handle. I grabbed a stepladder and the lights, and marched outside, but because I was only eight-years old and couldn't reach too high, I could only string the lights over our garage and front door. Without hooks, I improvised and took my mother's wooden clothespins and clipped the wires to the roof shingles. I was really proud of myself for being able to do this.

One evening before Christmas, I went caroling with a group of kids and some of their parents. When we arrived at my house, my mother came to the window to listen to us sing. As I looked up, I got a sinking feeling and felt ashamed because I thought everyone would notice the wooden clothespins and laugh. I was also worried that my drunken father would come to the door and embarrass me, as he had done on so many previous occasions. These are thoughts and feelings that should never have to occupy a young child's mind.

The effects of emotional, physical, or sexual abuse on a child can be devastating. Depending upon the nature and scope of the offense, children can develop a multitude of problems as they transition into adulthood. Children have different levels of resiliency depending upon their individual personality and the support they received from extended family members or positive role models outside the family. It's possible that there may be some children who endure abuse without developing any symptoms at all; however, abuse certainly increases the likelihood of developing psychological and health-related problems. Many studies have been conducted on the problems experienced by children from abusive backgrounds that you can research and review.

If you experienced extreme abuse or neglect in your own

childhood, you should definitely seek professional help and support as soon as possible. It is only by identifying and addressing the impacts of abuse that you are able to move beyond the role of the victim. The ultimate goal is to address and resolve your problems so that you can move on with your life without the emotional baggage of the past dragging you down.

Below is a long list of negative outcomes that children can develop. Although this list is overwhelming and can be intimidating or discouraging, remember you have the power to prevent yourself from developing any of these problems. You are not a statistic. You are a living, evolving, and powerful human being. You have the power of choice and with it the ability to change your destiny. Take some time to review these areas to determine which of them might be an area of concern for you.

- Depression and anxiety-related disorders
- Post-traumatic stress disorder
- Nightmares or inability to sleep
- Fear, guilt, or shame
- Low self-esteem
- Alcohol and substance abuse
- Nicotine addiction
- Financial problems
- Education and career problems
- Legal problems
- Relationship/marital problems

- Eating disorders, such as anorexia, bulimia, and obesity
- Aggressive behavior and anger issues
- Attention or concentration problems
- Social withdrawal or isolation
- Self-injury
- Suicide attempts
- Risky behavior
- Sexual identity problems
- Sexual promiscuity or dysfunction
- Sexually transmitted diseases
- Increased risks of hepatitis, diabetes, strokes, heart disease, high blood pressure, cancer, lung and liver disease, and other medical issues

Most of these problems are due to the many psychological, behavioral, and social experiences related to child abuse or maltreatment. These negative experiences tend to cause people to develop harmful behaviors and habits, such as smoking, drinking, drug use, high-risk sexual behaviors, and other negative lifestyle choices. These behaviors can then contribute to medical and health-related issues.

When you identify a problem area, don't let it overwhelm you. Instead, accept that this awareness is a good thing. You are becoming consciously aware of the effects your childhood had on you. You are recognizing and acknowledging your cognitive, behavioral, and emotional patterns, and this is offering you an opportunity to change.

View this period as a positive and exciting time. You are on a journey of self-discovery and reclaiming your power. You can begin to make healthy changes by taking action right now in this moment. You are even doing so by reading this book.

GROWTH TIPS

Explore and assess all the different areas of your life. Notice what's working well and where you need improvement. Identify the issues that are most troubling to you. Seek professional help and support.

CHAPTER THREE

"It's All Your Fault!"

"Take your life in your own hands, and what happens? A terrible thing: no one to blame."
—Erica Jong

When we recognize and come to accept that we were negatively affected by our childhoods, there is a natural tendency to blame our parents. Although our anger is valid, it needs to be managed and expressed in appropriate and meaningful ways. Playing the blame game only keeps us stuck in anger, resentment, and bitterness, which becomes way too consuming. Anger is usually the first emotion that hits us when something goes wrong. If we hold on to our anger for too long it turns into resentment, which is a much more persistent form of anger. Bitterness is a longstanding form of unresolved anger and resentment. It is the unhealthiest emotion to have because like a bad cancer, it eats away at the soul.

When troublesome childhood memories surface and problems of life arise, many people tend to blame their parents. Of course, it is much easier to place blame on others than it is to be responsible for the choices we make and the actions we take in our lives. If we didn't get the proper nurturing, love, and support from our parents or caregivers, it can certainly cause us to feel angry, resentful, and bitter.

For adults who were abused or neglected, blaming their parents is the easiest way to deal with emotions, justify negative behaviors, and make excuses for why their lives are so unsuccessful. The hardest thing for people to do is to face the past, address their issues, and come to terms with what happened to them as children.

Certainly, doing this work on yourself does not mean that you will suddenly develop incredible, loving relationships with your parents. This is more about reviewing your childhood experiences to understand and accept what happened to you. I encourage you to start keeping a journal to help you to sort out your emotions related to your experiences. You may want to write down any thoughts, feelings, reactions, or memories that resurface to gain insight. If you are engaged in psychotherapy or a support group, it can be helpful to discuss this in your counseling sessions. If not, perhaps you can explore it with a trusted friend or your spouse or significant other.

If you are still not comfortable talking about it with anyone, just sit with yourself and contemplate it for a while. What can you learn by making these connections to your past?

In order to gain an even broader perspective, it would also be helpful to learn about your parents' childhoods. Victims all tend to be victims of victims. Basically, abuse comes in a generational cycle. Abuse is passed down from parents to children. A child who is repeatedly verbally or physically abused, if left unchecked, will likely grow up to become a parent who exhibits the same type of abusive behaviors to his or her own children. What happened to your parents that caused them to behave so badly? In gaining greater insight and understanding you can begin to make deeper connections and put the pieces of the puzzle together.

Let me be clear. This advice is not meant to excuse or condone anyone's negative behavior or to minimize your painful experiences. Rather, it's about gaining greater clarity, understanding, and awareness so you can free yourself to live a happy, healthy, and successful life, and finally achieve your unshattered dreams.

When I explored my father's history many years ago, I learned that he was also an abused child. My father had a very strict father who always chastised him. My grandfather never demonstrated any love or affection towards my father and my father was subjected to severe abusive punishments when he did something that was perceived as "wrong" by my grandfather. My father struggled with low self-esteem and an untreated anxiety disorder throughout most of his adult life as a result of growing up in this abusive, oppressive environment. Unfortunately, he dealt with his pain in unhealthy and self-destructive ways, among them alcoholism, chain smoking, gambling, and other negative behaviors. Clearly, my father continued the generational cycle of abuse. He projected his anger outward in physically and emotionally abusive ways towards his family.

Knowledge of my father's upbringing allowed me to develop some empathy for him. As a young father, how could he give what he never received as a child? Furthermore, his generation was relatively unaware of abuse cycles, treatment, or counseling. Few people in the 1950s or 1960s went into psychotherapy to explore and resolve their emotional pain. There were no Oprahs or Dr. Phils on television talking about these problems either. People kept their matters to themselves. Psychotherapy was stigmatized and society expected you to just "deal with it," "toughen up," and, in the case of men, "be a man." Also, serving in the United States Army gave my father a tough exterior. He held the perception that *therapy is for wimps* and a sign of weakness. When I studied his life, I could see how tough it would have been for my father to heal from the pain of his childhood had he tried.

Unfortunately, when my mother tried to help my father enter into treatment or encouraged him to attend AA Meetings he mostly rejected the idea. He was in denial that he had a drinking problem, felt that AA was beneath him and said, "I can stop whenever I want to." He had a number of failed treatment attempts and did not make a conscious choice to change his behavior until it was too late for us as a family.

Sadly, many people who are abused or neglected as children often follow in the same footsteps as their parents as adults. While this is usually unintentional, it means they haven't done the necessary work on themselves to heal their pain from the past. As a result, most lack effective parenting skills and haven't learned how to manage their own emotional reactions. Nor do they know how to develop, support, and mentor their children. Consequently, they perpetuate a vicious cycle of abuse in their families.

The best way to prevent this from happening in your own household is to take ownership of yourself and your emotional reactions. Stop blaming your parents or other people in your life and take responsibility for your own actions. Although these painful experiences may be a part of your history, they do not have to dictate your future. These past events shaped you into the person you are today, and brought you to where you are in your life right now. But remember, you have also developed many positive and wonderful qualities from going through these experiences, so stop blaming yourself.

It is quite common for victims to blame themselves for the abuse they received. They frequently think that they are somehow responsible for the way they were treated. Consciously or unconsciously they feel that they were not good enough, smart enough, or pretty enough to deserve different treatment than they got, or they imagine that they were unlovable. This type of belief sometimes causes people to avoid really confronting the past because they may feel that they are somehow at fault.

Let me be crystal clear: You are not the cause of what happened to you. You were a helpless child and you must learn to forgive yourself now for any negative feelings you may have about yourself. Your parents or the people who mistreated you are the ones responsible for what happened. They are the ones who made the choices that caused you unhappiness, pain, and/or trauma. You are not to blame for anything.

Please don't allow blame to interfere with your personal growth and development any longer. If you do, you will only waste precious time and remain trapped in the past and consumed by negativity. You will continue to hold on to anger, resentment, and bitterness that will taint and diminish the rest of your life.

Open your mind to the possibilities that healing and recovery can offer you. Focus your thoughts and attention on what can happen in the future, not on what happened in the past. Reclaim your power! You are no longer a victim of your parents and your early life experiences. You have chosen to embark on an exciting journey of self-healing and discovery that can lead you to a wonderful new life. As you develop yourself, you will learn to become a kinder, loving, more responsible, and more compassionate person. You will increase your confidence and self-esteem, and develop an inner strength that you never before knew existed.

When you truly accept that blaming your parents is counterproductive, you can begin to make positive changes and open yourself up to a whole new world of possibilities, like:

- Being free to explore the future.
- Reclaiming your personal power and control over yourself.
- Making a profound difference in your own life and the lives of others.

Take the time you need to evaluate your childhood circumstances. Although you may never fully understand why you had to go through all of these experiences, you can certainly learn from them. Begin to let go and stop dwelling on past events that keep you from the happiness you so richly deserve. When you do, you will be able to create the life you were truly meant to live.

There is absolutely no excuse for the pain you endured as a child. I know that you suffered, and you have every right to your feelings about it. But in order to move forward, you must stop the blame, release the past, and choose to turn your life around. Only you can do this, and now you know you have the choice. Don't continue to dwell on childhood negativity. Take the things that hurt you and transcend them. Vow to break the generational cycle of abuse in your family and learn how to become a better parent, sibling, friend, spouse, lover, employee, business owner, citizen, and person.

GROWTH TIPS

Stop blaming your parents for the life you are currently living. Reclaim your power by releasing the past. Gain insight and understanding about your experiences and about your parents' childhoods. Turn your life around and become an inspiration to others.

CHAPTER FOUR

Releasing the Past Through Forgiveness

"Forgiveness is the fragrance that the violet sheds on the heel that has crushed it."
—Mark Twain

To let go of the past, we must be willing to forgive others and ourselves. Forgiveness is not always an easy concept to grasp and we tend to resist it. Most people believe that if they forgive someone they are allowing themselves to remain victimized and powerless over the person who caused them harm. They feel that forgiveness condones the person's behavior. This is a paradox, however, because it's actually the opposite that's true. When we forgive someone we release our emotional attachment to that person and to the past. When we forgive ourselves, we empower ourselves to move forward with our lives. Forgiveness really does equate to freedom.

Yes, you may have been wronged by someone and your anger may be entirely justified. Therefore it's important to acknowledge and fully understand your feelings before you can be ready to forgive. Taking the time to work through your anger and hurt will give you an opportunity to express your feelings about what you experienced. This allows you to gain a healthier perspective on the situation and you will eventually be more receptive to the idea of forgiveness.

It also helps if you can understand the feelings and experiences of the person who offended you. By giving the other person a chance to explain why he or she behaved that way, you will have an opportunity to obtain greater insight into the situation and learn what his or her motives were. Perhaps, you were hurt unintentionally as a result of someone's own inner pain, or perhaps there was a misunderstanding. You will never really know until you are able to gain clarity about it.

In certain unique situations it might be helpful to communicate with the person who hurt you. Of course this is not always possible or may not even be good for you to do, and you will have to seek resolution in other ways.

Without a healthy dose of forgiveness, though, you can't hope to make any real progress.

Ultimately forgiveness is really more about forgiving yourself than about forgiving those who harmed you. You may not be ready or able to forgive because you can't forget what happened and there is no reason to forgive anyone anyway. Although you may develop some empathy and understanding for those who made your childhood difficult, you shouldn't be expected to forgive their actions. The important distinction here is that you can offer forgiveness to the person because you have a greater understanding about their limitations and their own inner pain, but you are not condoning or forgiving the behavior or actions that harmed you.

Again, this is really about forgiving yourself. You may still be carrying a personal sense of blame or responsibility for what happened to you as a child. Until you forgive yourself and accept that you were not the cause of the problem, you will find yourself unconsciously holding on to a sense of guilt and responsibility that will keep you from making any real progress.

When the unthinkable happens, we look for answers in an attempt to gain understanding and control of the situation. Of course, no children are responsible for their parents' abusive behavior; however, it is common for children to feel as if they did something wrong or that they should have done something different to prevent the abuse from happening. Children tend to blame themselves for the horrors they have endured. Some will even believe that they were bad and deserved it.

Even when we grow older and realize these are inaccurate reactions, they are still a part of our past. The old thoughts and memories linger and they continue to impact us every day. There are many intelligent and accomplished adults who survived difficult childhoods who still have thoughts of responsibility and blame. If this sounds like you, then please recognize right now that it's time to let this go and accept, once and for all, that you were not responsible for what happened to you. There are no easy answers as to why you had to suffer, but it certainly had nothing to do with anything you did to cause it. You did not deserve to be treated as you were!

I know I am stressing this point, but I really want to drive it home. Until you finally come to grips with the fact that you were a helpless child who was powerless in the past, and forgive yourself, you will remain stuck and your progress will be slow. Forgive yourself for anything you think you did or may have done as a child. None of it warranted what happened to you.

Forgive yourself for the unproductive years of self-blame, too. You merely reacted in predictable and normal ways to a horrible situation. Your reactions were instinctive and natural. You did nothing wrong. Holding on to thoughts of guilt, shame, or regret won't help you.

Focus your energies on what you can do now to minimize the residual effects of the abuse you endured. This is something for which you can take responsibility. Progress begins with understanding, and part of that understanding involves acknowledging and accepting that no child, including you, is ever responsible for a painful childhood. Forgive yourself and you'll be one step closer to finding ways to get closure and resolution of your past.

I didn't speak to my father for seven years after my parents finally ended their relationship. I was a teenager working my way through college at Toys "R" Us. I remember observing many children who came into the store with their fathers. They looked so happy and excited to be there together as they shopped for new playthings. I felt a huge void inside of me because I had never had that same type of closeness with my father. I never had positive memories to hold on to and it bothered me. I had a lot of anger and pain that I still needed to work through.

During this time, I knew that my father got remarried and had another child with his new spouse. Every Christmas he sent gifts to me and my siblings. My brother and I were very angry and we always sent them back because we wanted nothing to do with him. I also heard that he had stopped drinking and I just couldn't understand why he was never able to do this when we were a family. The anger and pain cut deeply and I had a lot of burning questions that went unanswered. As I worked through these feelings in therapy, I embarked on a path of forgiveness. I realized that I needed to do this in order to move on with my life.

Eventually I contacted my father and scheduled some time to meet with him. I asked him a lot of questions about our past and about his childhood. I wanted to know why he treated us the way he did. I also asked him a lot of questions about his current life and wondered if he was happy. I came to realize that my father had a lot of unresolved issues that still bothered him. I also recognized his limited ability to communicate his true feelings. I learned more about my father in that brief meeting than I had ever known. I made a conscious choice to forgive him and attempted to mend our relationship.

This ultimately led to a dinner reunion one evening at my father's house. My brother, sister, and I went to my father's home, where we met his new wife and our half-sister. During this time, my mother and I were living together, and she struggled hard to make ends meet. We lived in an affordable four-room apartment she was able to obtain in the housing projects in Queens. My father was always erratic with his alimony payments and he never paid any child support that was legally due to us. I had quite a reaction when I saw how differently my father was living. The contrast was unbelievable to me. My father lived in a huge estate home in an exclusive neighborhood on Long Island. As I toured this incredible house, I felt a sickening pain in my gut and felt bad for my mother at the injustice of it all.

Although we reunited and I tried to renew my relationship with my father over the years, it ultimately didn't
have the ending I'd hoped for. The process freed me emotionally though. I learned many life lessons and gained
insights into the past that I never would have if I hadn't
gone through this experience.

It takes a lot of courage to confront and deal with the
past. Don't ignore it or push it away, because it won't help
you or release you from despair. By facing the past and
dealing with it squarely, you will find a renewed sense of
strength within you. Through forgiveness you reclaim
your personal power and your parents finally lose any remaining power they may hold over you.

Basically, you have three choices about how to deal with
your past. You can deny it, stuff your emotions, and try
to push it away. You can think about it constantly, blame
others, and hold on to anger, resentment and bitterness
that will hinder your ability to live a happy and fulfilled
life. Or you can accept what happened, recognize you
were powerless as a child, forgive, and release the past.

Clearly, the last choice is the best choice. Accepting, forgiving, and moving on with your life are the most important things you can do to free yourself. Forgiveness enables you to release the emotional bonds of the past and
allows you to take personal accountability for yourself
and your life.

Imagine the kind of life you can live when you accept the fact that you can never change what happened and you let go of the past. You finally put it behind you and step fully into the present.

Forgiveness is an indication of personal growth and responsibility. Once you are able to forgive, you can stop the blame. You understand that blaming others has kept you from being fully accountable for your life today and creating the future you desire. Through forgiveness, you may realize that you were only using blame to protect yourself and to make excuses for why your life is not the way you want it to be. When you are able to forgive, you can begin an adventure of exploring your mind and learning what really matters to you. You can embark on a journey of self-discovery and learn new ways to enjoy life. Forgiveness allows you to release the past and embrace the future with a newfound sense of emotional freedom.

GROWTH TIPS

Be open and willing to forgive yourself, the past, and the people who hurt you. Remember forgiveness does not condone a person's behavior or actions. Take time to work through your emotions related to past events. Attempt to gain a broader perspective on the situation and the person (or persons) who wronged you. Release the past and embrace your future with a newfound sense of emotional freedom.

CHAPTER FIVE

Self-parenting, Learning to Love Yourself, and Self-acceptance

*"You must love yourself before you love another.
By accepting yourself and fully being what you are,
your simple presence can make others happy."*
—Mignon McLaughlin

O nce you recognize and acknowledge the painful aspects of your childhood and you have taken the steps to heal yourself through forgiveness, you will start to realize that there are many needs you had as a child that will never be fulfilled. These are sometimes known as frozen needs, any unmet childhood need that is carried into adulthood. A frozen need is basically a void that a person feels they need to fill in other ways. Oftentimes trying to fill a void within oneself leads to addictive or compulsive behaviors, such as shopping, gambling, casual sex, and so on. Of course, the need can never be satisfied because it is masking an unsatisfied frozen need that was missed out on in childhood.

It is very painful to realize that these childhood needs will not be fulfilled, and you will most likely go through a period of mourning over them. You can, however, attend to some of these unmet needs in healthy ways through self-parenting, learning how to love yourself, and self-acceptance. Start to give yourself some of the things you never received as a child, which will begin to soften and melt some of those frozen needs.

As adults, we typically treat ourselves and others in the same way we were treated by our parents. We internalized the parenting styles of our parents or other caregivers and their voices still resonate in our heads. Even if we consciously try to counter these patterns, in times of stress we easily fall right back into them because we are unconsciously familiar with these habits. This is why you often hear people say, "Oh my God . . . I sound just like my mother," when they catch themselves reprimanding their children.

Furthermore, we frequently gravitate towards similar

people or circumstances that match our early childhood experiences. Rooted deep in our unconscious is a desire to mend the primary relationship we had with the parent who wounded us. We want the parent's love and acceptance and we want to make the story turn out all right. Subsequently, as adults we tend to look for people who will do exactly what was done to us in the past.

This means, if you were verbally and emotionally abused, you might find yourself hearing the same phrases and feeling exactly as you did when you were a child. If you were abandoned, you may begin relationships with people who are likely to abandon you, or to interpret behavior as abandonment. If you were hurt physically, you may create situations in which you can experience this again. These repetitive patterns will most likely occur with different people and circumstances, causing you to wonder, *Why do I do this over and over again?*

Until you resolve your unconscious core patterns you will continue to recreate the same types of circumstances that are disturbing to you. The good news is that you can change and prevent this from happening. Yes, it takes time, awareness, and determination to resolve a core pattern, but it can be done. One of the ways you can start to alter these patterns is to learn how to self-parent and love yourself. This means that you can treat yourself in ways that a healthy parent would treat a child. Refer back to Chapter 2 for details on some of the qualities and skills of effective parenting, and then start giving them to yourself.

Do you put yourself down or berate yourself if you make a mistake? Are you overly critical of yourself? Do you constantly push yourself to do more or strive to improve, but never feel that you are good enough? Do you minimize your successes as if they aren't important or don't really mean that much? Do you compare yourself to other people and feel that you always come up empty? Do you ever feel that you are unworthy? If you are like most people from a difficult childhood, you probably answered yes to many or all of these questions. If so, you need to identify these internal thought patterns so that they can be eliminated.

Here are some ideas to get you started:

- Begin to recognize when you repeat a past pattern. Tune in to how you feel, as this is an indication of your current thoughts. Do you have a sinking or upset feeling because you believe you are a bad or awful person who is not good enough? Explore what you are going through in the moment to determine if there is anything actually happening in your life right now that is reinforcing this feeling. The current event may merely be triggering past thoughts, emotions, and feelings.
- Consider your relationship dynamics with your parents. How did you react or behave around

them when you were a child or an adolescent?
What did you think about yourself and how did
you feel? It can be helpful to write down some of
your reactions to these experiences in your journal. What were your thoughts and feelings about
it? How did you behave as a result? Did you get
angry and fight back or become quiet and hide?
Doing this can help you gain objectivity about
it. You can also discuss these experiences with
your therapist if you have one or a loved one who
supports you.

- Write about what it was like to be a child at
  different ages: five-years old, eight-years old, six-
  teen-years old, and so on. What was your home
  life like? What was an average day like? Who
  were you connected to? Who loved and supported you, and how did they show it? What did you
  do, think or feel when you were mistreated?

- Review your journal entries to see if there are
  any parallels between your past and present
  thoughts, feelings, and behaviors.

- Write daily journal entries to stay conscious of
  your thoughts, patterns, concerns, behaviors,
  and life events. You will have this to refer back to
  later on, and it will help to clarify any confusion
  between your past and current reality.

- Learn healthy parenting strategies and integrate
  them for yourself. What does it mean to be a
  good parent? Demonstrate these loving supportive qualities to your inner child who was abused,

abandoned, or neglected.

- Explore inner child work and resources, such as
  the books and audio programs of John Bradshaw
  and Louise Hay.

As an adult, you can become your own loving parent to the child who still lives within you. Loving yourself is the primary ingredient in self-parenting and inner child work. Loving yourself can be difficult when you have limiting and derogatory messages still playing in your unconscious mind. Again, most of these messages were absorbed and recorded during childhood and they have detrimental effects. You are still being influenced by the messages your parents and others gave to you years ago. When you were told you were no good, and that you would never amount to anything, did you believe it? When you were told you were stupid or weird did you believe that, too?

Even if you are consciously aware of these underlying beliefs you may still hold on to them today. It is possible to erase and change these limiting beliefs and you can start by learning to love yourself. As much of a cliché as this sounds, you need to be reminded of it again and again: The most important person to learn to love is yourself. Find ways to love, nurture, and support yourself. Do things that bring you joy. Be gentle and kind to yourself—always. Your relationships with others will grow out of the loving relationship and sense of appreciation you develop for yourself. The people you come into contact with will be greatly influenced by your presence and they will respond to the love emanating from within you.

Here are some ways to help you to love and accept yourself.

Romance yourself. Think about the last person you fell in love with. When the relationship began, you probably devoted a lot of time, energy, attention, and care to this person. You were passionate, swept away, and wanted to be near them all the time. Why not enter into a similar process and create a loving, joyful relationship with yourself? Learn to appreciate who you are and enjoy your own company.

Remember, other people can leave you, but you will never leave yourself. You are the only person you will ever be with on a constant basis throughout every day of your life, so why not create the most incredible relationship you can with yourself? Do things that make you happy. Treat yourself to nice things, and be kind to yourself. You deserve to be treated in incredibly loving ways.

Become your own best friend. If you really want to live a happier life, believing that you can succeed and having confidence in yourself is essential. For if you don't believe in yourself, how can you expect others to believe in you? Yes, it's true that you have gone through rough times in your life, but remember: No matter what you've been through, you can choose to support yourself in overcoming these obstacles. Now is the time to become your own best friend.

Emphasize your good qualities. When your self-esteem and self-confidence are low, you'll tend to focus on the negative aspects of yourself while minimizing your positive qualities. Turn this around by praising and encouraging yourself in order to develop positive self-regard. When you accomplish a task, congratulate yourself. Tell yourself, "I'm really proud of myself for doing that!" Acknowledge and celebrate your successes. This supports you in loving yourself and being your own best friend.

Examine your beliefs. You probably still have a lot of old limiting beliefs and internalized messages that you are not fully aware of. In order to discover the beliefs that are holding you back, you can go back to your journal and write some of them down. Take time to reflect back on an earlier time in your life and see if you can discover when and how a belief you uncover got started. Give yourself some prompts, with statements such as: "My earliest memory of being called stupid is . . . ," "My mother (or father) always made me feel . . . ," "My mother (or father) always treated me like . . .," and so on. Write down whatever thoughts, feelings, or memories a statement like these evokes in you.

Then, begin to question and challenge your beliefs. Are they really true? Were they ever true? In what context was the message sent to you? Make a decision to replace negative and limiting beliefs with new beliefs that you want to be true for you. Remember, a belief is just a thought you keep thinking, and you can always choose to change your thoughts. This is where your power lies. Learn to write and speak affirmations to replace the old limiting beliefs and focus on your new and improved statements until you believe them to be true.

Developing Your Own Affirmations

Here are some tips to help you develop effective affirmations on your own.

- Keep your affirmations in the present tense. An affirmation is much more effective when it is stated in the present tense. For example: "I now have a wonderful new apartment" vs. "I am going to have a wonderful new apartment."
- Stay positive. State what you want rather than what you don't want. "I am now thin and attractive" instead of "I don't want to be fat."
- Keep your affirmations short and to the point. Simple, direct statements have a greater impact upon the subconscious mind than long, wordy sentences do. They are also easier to write and remember.
- Repetition is important. Your subconscious mind will be imprinted with your positive affirmations faster if you frequently repeat them.
- Connect your affirmations to your emotions. Really feel the emotions behind the words you are saying. Don't just say your affirmations by rote.

When speaking your affirmations really feel them in the core of your being.

- Be consistent. The more you practice your affirmations the better your results will be.
- Belief matters. Develop affirmations that you can believe in. It's important to believe that the affirmations are possible, otherwise the mind tends to shut them down.
- Personalize your affirmations. Use "I" statements and even include your name in some of your affirmations too. When you say: "I, Jane Doe, am a beautiful person both inside and out," it makes your affirmation much more powerful because you hear the wonderful sound of your own name!

Affirmations may not feel right at first, but if you repeat them for a month or so on a daily basis, you will come to accept them because they feel so much better. Allow yourself to feel good. You deserve it! Change your thoughts and beliefs and watch your life improve for the better.

One of the books that had a profound influence on me as I went through the process of healing from my own difficult childhood in my early twenties was the book *You Can Heal Your Life* by Louise Hay. The book provides various exercises using affirmations and mirror work to teach you to love and approve of yourself and to connect with your inner child. I used a lot of Hay's exercises and found them very helpful. This is a book I highly recommend.

The primary thoughts you think and the words you speak

will determine how you ultimately feel about yourself. It's important to interrupt your negative thought patterns by catching yourself when you are going down what I call the "negative highway." Begin by paying attention to what you think throughout the day. Is most of it positive or negative? When you catch yourself, try to examine the negative thought or belief and challenge it. Test it against your current reality. Is it really true?

Stop criticizing yourself and putting yourself down. Do you always say negative things like, "I'm an idiot" or "That was such a stupid thing to do" or "I'm ugly"? The way you perceive yourself comes out in what you say and do. If you catch yourself saying such things, stop right away and correct yourself. What you say to yourself can change how you view yourself and the world, and will influence your behavior and actions, so it's important not to criticize.

Use positive affirmations to support yourself in everything you do. When you're getting ready for the day, look in the mirror. Acknowledge your positive qualities and characteristics, and say them out loud.

Say phrases into the mirror, such as:

- "I am an attractive person."
- "I am a good person."
- "I love myself."
- "I look really good in these clothes."
- "I am brilliant."

Again, even if you don't fully believe these statements right now, say them anyway! You'll soon realize that they become the truth for you. You can also post positive quotes or affirmations where you can see them throughout the day to help keep you focused.

No matter what's stopping you from believing in yourself and loving yourself, there's a way to overcome it. First you need to identify what's causing your self-doubt. Is it fear, insecurity, a poor mental attitude, or something else? Once identified, then can you face the obstacle and overcome it.

Here are some more positive affirmations to help you love and accept yourself. Take a look at the samples below and use them if they resonate with you. If not, try changing them slightly until they trigger the mindset and emotional state you want to achieve.

- "I am filled with love, peace, and joy."
- "I treat myself with kindness and respect."
- "I release the need to be perfect and accept myself just the way I am."
- "I give myself permission to shine."
- "I honor the best parts of myself and share them with others."
- "I'm proud of all I have accomplished."
- "Today, I give myself permission to be greater than my fears."
- "I love myself no matter what."

- "I am my own best friend and I support myself in all that I do."
- "I am grateful for all the qualities, traits, and talents that make me unique."

Self-confident people recognize and acknowledge their skills and capabilities. Even so, some people, especially those who lack confidence, find this difficult to do because they feel as if they are bragging or acting egotistical when they do. In truth, you don't actually have to brag to give yourself credit. Even the humblest person takes some time to appreciate what he or she has to offer to the world.

GROWTH TIPS

Identify your positive qualities and begin to appreciate yourself for them. If you cannot come up with one good thing you like about yourself, use your journal to log your daily activities and track what you do each day. You will eventually identify some incredible traits, skills, talents, and abilities you possess that have a positive impact upon the people and world around you. By using your journal in this way, it serves like a mirror, reflecting back to you all your good qualities, including those which otherwise would go unnoticed by you normally.

A journal is a great tool to put some proof in front of your eyes. It reinforces what you are doing and helps you get accustomed to feeling good about yourself.

CHAPTER SIX

Who Supports You?

"Success depends on the support of other people.
The only hurdle between you and what you want to
be is in the support of other people."
—David Joseph Schwartz

There is a tendency for children from abusive backgrounds always to go it alone. We were taught to keep quiet and not tell others what was happening at home. We may have also been threatened with harm to ourselves or the people we loved if we dared to tell anyone.

Do any of these phrases sound familiar to you?

- "Keep your mouth shut."
- "Don't air your dirty laundry in public."
- "People don't want to hear about your problems."
- "If you tell anyone, you're gonna get it."
- "This is nobody's business."
- "What happens in the family stays in the family."

These negative and restrictive messages became embedded in our subconscious minds and caused us to remain isolated in our pain. We learned to distrust others, remained silent, and kept to ourselves.

As you face your childhood and reflect on the things that caused you pain, you may realize that you need help and support. Remember, no one is an island! Initially, you may find that only professional psychotherapy can help. In extreme cases of abuse it is imperative that you get help from a trained professional. No book alone can help you to heal and therefore you will need the support and insight of a trained therapist to help you resolve these issues. You may also benefit from joining a support group with other people who have had similar experiences.

You no longer have to remain silent and isolated in pain and sorrow. Once you open up and take the risk to trust others, you will feel a sense of relief.

Some people have childhood memories that are not as severe. They may not necessarily require professional counseling, but they can still benefit from the support of friends, family, teachers, life coaches, and support groups. People who know and understand what you went through can get you to focus on the issues at hand and help you to move forward in your life. People who care about you will be more than willing to assist, however, please be cautious about whom you disclose your personal information to. Make sure that it is someone you can trust and someone who has your best interests in mind. Positive and nurturing people can support you in overcoming the challenges of the past as you regain personal power over your life. Finding appropriate support is critical on your journey.

Here are some of the types of people who can help.

- Therapists/mental health counselors
- Medical doctors
- Employee assistance program (EAP) counselors
- Clergy
- Spouses or significant others
- Teachers
- Life coaches
- Friends
- Family
- Support groups

Start by confiding in someone you trust. After sharing the details of your experiences and your feelings (only to the degree you are comfortable), ask for their support in guiding you to the appropriate resources.

Positive people will gladly encourage and support you, whereas negative people will tell you that you can't achieve your goals. They tell you to "be realistic" and that what you want is just too hard or impossible to obtain. Don't listen to them!

If you're holding on to beliefs that perpetuate negative thought patterns, then you will most likely bring more negativity into your life. If you find yourself focusing on the negative aspects of your life, such as your difficult childhood, physical ailments, or unfulfilling relationships, then you need to make a change. If not, you will use this negativity as an excuse for why you can't have the life you want.

As a child from a difficult background, you absorbed a lot of negative criticism instead of encouragement. The negative messages you received from your parents are probably still playing in your head. Perhaps you have always surrounded yourself with negative people because this is what you have come to expect from life or what you unconsciously feel you deserve—or because you think everyone is this way. It seems more natural for you to accept these toxic people into your life because they fit into your emotional comfort level.

Whatever the reason, it's time to break the cycle of negativity. Consider raising your standard of expectation. Find people to associate with who emit positive energy, people who love and appreciate you for who you are.

When seeking other positive people, think of those you most admire and identify traits they have that you especially enjoy. Use these individuals as role models and start to develop some of these traits and qualities within yourself. You will usually be drawn to people who have a similar personality or hold the same set of values as you.

Here are some ways that will help you connect to positive people, and create more joyful energy in your life.

- Focus on the positive qualities in other people. It's far easier to see someone's faults before seeing their goodness. Challenge yourself to look only for the good in people.
- Recognize your finest attributes and put them out into the world. Not only will this contribute to your self-awareness and increase your self-esteem, but people will respond to you in like ways.
- Exercise compassion, especially showing it to yourself. Negative energy causes us to obsess about our faults and the goals we have not attained. Positive energy allows us to realize that we are doing the best we can. Be kind to yourself.
- Value other people's opinions. Positive energy is open minded. Listen to all points of view and do your best to understand them, regardless of how different they might be from your own. Trying to change someone's mind is usually futile, so, *even if you're right*, save your energy, understand their opinion, and move on.

- Stop judging. Give others and yourself the benefit of the doubt. Negative energy is critical and judgmental. Judging only focuses on faults and produces more negative energy. This will usually attract more of the same back to you.
- Be honest. Express your true self in thoughts, words, and actions.
- Accept your imperfections. You will definitely have negative thoughts and emotions on occasion. We're all human, and negative thoughts are a part of human nature. The key is to redirect them and not dwell on them.
- Celebrate the success and happiness of others. Negative energy is jealous, but positive people are thrilled when others succeed. Use someone else's success as a motivator to make you a better person.
- Balance fulfillment of your own needs and desires with the service you give to others. If you spend your life trying to please others, you may find yourself ignoring your own needs. Positive energy is balanced.
- Persevere in spite of fear or defeat. We all experience defeat and disappointment from time to time. Rather than allowing a setback to keep you from reaching your goals, use it as a chance to learn something new and prepare for your next challenge.
- Follow your unshattered dreams and desires. Embrace joy every step along the way. You are

on a journey to achieving your goals. How exciting is that?

As a young boy, I was gregarious and social. I always had
a lot of friends in the neighborhood that I enjoyed playing
and interacting with. I had a natural desire to explore and
involve myself in social activities. In elementary school,
I did my first musical, *The Music Man*, and I caught the
acting bug. When my parents divorced and we lost our
home and relocated to live in my aunt's basement apartment, I was taken away from my network of friends and
felt abandoned. I was only twelve-years old and this was
quite traumatic.

As I mentioned earlier, when we moved I went into a state
of culture shock and withdrew inwardly. I didn't know
anyone in the new neighborhood except for my cousin who lived a few miles away. There weren't many kids
my age in the area and I became isolated and lonely. In a
sense, I didn't even want to make new friends or get close
to anyone because I figured I would eventually be taken
away from them too. I put up walls to protect myself. I
also felt a lot of shame about my father and my home life
and I didn't want anyone to know about it. I kept quiet
and withdrew into a fantasy world. Frequently, I aimless-
ly wandered the streets alone and sang to myself, while
dreaming about becoming famous someday.

One Sunday, there was a casting call in the local church
bulletin for the musical *Damn Yankees*. I decided to au-

dition and I got a part. I was so thrilled to be a part of something I loved and wanted to do. Although I was shy and insecure, I received a lot of positive attention for my acting and piano playing, and this made me feel worthy.

Of course, my father made fun of my theatrical ambitions. He told me I would never make it in show business because I wasn't good enough, and this hurt me very deeply. I usually tried to ignore his negative comments and got defensive with an attitude of *I'll show you.* Somehow I had some level of belief in myself, and being around positive people in a venue I loved provided me with a sense of validation. I also felt that I was moving closer toward my goal of becoming an actor.

Even though I was young, inhibited, and intimidated around the other cast members, being in a creative environment made me feel good. It also gave me a sense of connection and belonging.

It is of utmost importance to surround yourself with positive people who encourage and support you to express your talents and capabilities. Positive people approach the world with an open heart and a sense of humor. They refuse to be tainted by cynicism and bitterness. They strive to see the best in the world around them, revel in the success of others, and diligently pursue their own goals and dreams. Becoming a positive person will help you to attract healthier people into your life. The more positive people that surround you, the more joy, contentment, and fulfillment you will experience in your own life.

Human beings are social creatures and we need to be connected to one another. One of the best ways to develop this connection is through friends. Friendships are one of the most important relationships we will ever have as human beings. Without friends, we feel lonely, rejected, and disconnected. Even in a marriage or partnership, we need friends outside of the relationship to fulfill our social needs or help us through difficult situations. Building meaningful friendships takes loyalty, trust, and honesty and it takes time.

Most people have meaningful friendships with only a handful of people at most. True friendships take work and they are more about quality than quantity. Yes, you can have several friends, but many of them will be more like acquaintances rather than true friends because the relationship lacks a deeper connection. Being a true friend requires some sacrifice. In a meaningful friendship, we may sometimes be asked to give up our own desires to meet our friend's needs. This may not always be so convenient for us. For instance, our friend may be ill and need us in the middle of the night. This would involve sacrificing the comfort of a good night's sleep in a nice, warm bed in order to be there for our friend. But we don't mind, because that's what friends are for!

In a meaningful friendship, there is a natural give and take. Mutual feelings exist and the relationship is never one sided. This doesn't mean that there won't ever be conflicts. Let's face it, we're human. However, when a conflict arises between two very close friends, the struggles usually don't last very long if each person chooses to forgive, understand, and communicate with one another. When a friendship is truly meaningful, the relationship is real; there are no facades, masks, or secrets. There is mutual honesty, sincerity, loyalty, and trust, which continue to grow as the friendship evolves.

Be willing to develop friendships. You may have recently met someone new by chance, at work, or through another friend. If there is enough common interest, you may decide to see the person again. With each encounter, your relationship grows and strengthens. As you continue to get to know one another, the communication becomes easier and you feel more comfortable and relaxed with one other. This is a natural process that takes some time. If you try to force a relationship, the other person may get uncomfortable and feel threatened, which will cause them to back away. So start off slowly and go at a smooth and steady pace. Let things take their course and evolve naturally.

As a new friendship grows, you will build trust and loyalty through the joys and difficulties of life. It's in the difficult times that a person's true colors are revealed. When you're going through a personal crisis, or simply a rough patch, it's the true friends who are there to help you through it. True friends help each other grow mentally, physically, emotionally, and spiritually. Building a meaningful friendship takes time to achieve, but once you develop a true friendship you will definitely know that it is worth the risk.

GROWTH TIPS

Seek out support and allow yourself to talk about what happened to you as a child. Locate professional resources and support groups to help you transcend your past. Get involved in social activities that make you happy and allow you to feel good and utilize your talents. Develop healthy and loving friendships with positive people who respect and value you.

CHAPTER SEVEN

The Courage to Change

*"It takes a lot of courage to release the familiar
and seemingly secure, to embrace the new.
But there is no real security in what is no longer
meaningful. There is more security in the
adventurous and exciting, for in movement there
is life, and in change there is power."*
—Alan Cohen

Ilove this quote because it encourages us to reach for more than we think we are capable of. It also poses the opposite view to what most of us believe. Many people think that security lies in the familiar and routine, but they rarely examine the costs of staying the same.

The truth is that life is constantly in flux and things are always changing. The more we accept and embrace this truth, the better our lives become, because we can choose to be proactive and initiate positive changes in our lives. To do this, we must own our power and direct our thoughts, intentions, and actions in deliberate ways.

Try it for yourself. This is when you are living from a higher state of consciousness and life gets good!

People resist change for various reasons, but the primary reason is fear. We're afraid of uncertainty and the unknown. The life we're living may not be great, but with it at least we know what we have and we're used to it. The problem with operating out of fear is that we limit our potential. We prevent ourselves from taking risks, going for what we want, and living larger lives.

At this point you know that the only way to move forward in your life is to address your childhood issues so that you can put them in perspective and resolve the past. Obviously, going back to review painful childhood experiences can be extremely frightening. It is not an easy thing to do. It takes a lot of strength and courage to look at the parts of yourself that you would rather not see. This is why you need a good therapist and positive people in your life to support you.

There is a fear factor involved in looking back because exploring emotional wounds makes us vulnerable. Fear is an extremely powerful emotion that can be paralyzing. It stands in the way of progress because it generally seems much easier to avoid and deny frightening or uncomfortable situations than to face them head on. As discussed earlier, this can cause us to react by developing a variety of self-destructive behaviors to avoid our pain. Overcoming fear though is the only way to get ourselves to the point where we can begin to understand a difficult childhood and emerge from its grip.

You must be willing to take risks to move beyond your comfort zone to go forward in life. This applies to every life area, not only in dealing with your childhood. One of my favorite quotes on risk taking is by Leo Buscaglia, Ph.D. If you are unfamiliar with his work, I definitely encourage you to read some of his books. Dr. Buscaglia was a philosopher, motivational speaker, and professor who taught classes on love, and he wrote many wonderful books on relationships and the art of loving.

In his book *Living, Loving and Learning* (Ballantine, 1982), Dr. Buscaglia writes, "The person who risks nothing, does nothing, has nothing, is nothing, and becomes nothing. He may avoid suffering and sorrow, but he simply cannot learn and feel and change and grow and love and live. Chained by his certitude, he is a slave; he has forfeited his freedom. Only the person who risks is truly free."

What does this quote mean to you?

What risks might you be avoiding and how does this impact your life?

Presently, I am putting myself out there in numerous ways and on different levels in my work as a coach. In the fall of 2011, I was approached about doing a live radio show at a premier radio station in New York City. At first I was skeptical and thought, *Come on, is this for real? I've never done radio before. I'm not sure how to do this.* The doubts and fears came rising to the surface. Now, what do you think would have happened if I had made a decision based on that type of thinking? I would have probably stopped myself, said no, and closed the door on a great opportunity.

When dealing with fear or anxiety, it's often best to start with where you are and proceed within your present level of comfort. It's a bit like taking baby steps or getting your feet wet to test the water. It can be helpful to simply gather more information and then make an informed decision. There's really no harm in doing that, and breaking things down into smaller steps reduces the fear and anxiety associated with doing anything new. So that's exactly what I did. I scheduled a meeting with the radio station, learned what was involved in hosting a show, asked about the contractual requirements, and ultimately made the decision to do it.

Fear is the thing that holds us back the most. It could be fear of failure, fear of success, or fear of the unknown.

For everyone the fear is different. The one thing that I have learned is that your *desire* must be stronger than your fear. So with my radio show example, I said yes and took the risk because my *desire* to try something new, my *desire* to challenge myself and use my creativity in a new way, and my *desire* to reach people in a larger venue were stronger than my fear of never having done a radio show before.

To take it a step further, I can honestly say that having had the experience of dealing with the emotions of moving through fear and beyond my comfort zone has made it much easier to take future risks in my life and business.

The point is, you never really know where risk taking can lead you. It might not always work out the way you hoped or expected, but there is always a lesson to be learned and something to be gained from the experience. I encourage you to start taking some risks to move beyond the comfort zone in your life.

To give you a visual image of this: Take a moment to grab a pen and some paper. Draw a circle on the page and put a dot in the middle of the circle. The dot represents you. When you are standing inside the circle, you're in your comfort zone. Now this may be fine for you. You may like it there, it might be cozy, but if you stay within the inner circle for too long you'll begin to stagnate because you have never challenged yourself to grow.

As you move toward the outer edge of the circle, you get closer to making a change. When you break through the cutting edge to the other side you move outside of your comfort zone. You might feel a bit scared, anxious, or disoriented—if so, remind yourself that this is only a temporary thing. Once you make the transition, and begin to adjust to new circumstances, people, and events, you will develop a new comfort zone.

That's how you grow throughout your life. There is a learning curve involved, and you need to be patient with yourself. The real key, however, is to make sure that your goal is not too far out of the range of your existing comfort zone, as this can cause you too much anxiety. When a goal is too big your energy is more focused on dealing with anxiety than on fulfilling your actual goal. So you want to be in a place where you're very excited and a little bit scared at the same time. You know it's a stretch, but you are confident that you can handle it and then you go for it. That's growth and change!

Yes, rehashing childhood experiences can be frightening, but please don't let this stop you from doing it. It is time to face your fears and release the past. Doing nothing about it is far more detrimental to you in the long run. This is your life we're talking about! Take some time to really think about what's been holding you back from addressing your childhood difficulties to find closure. Make a commitment to yourself by deciding to do something about it. Once you move through fear and take action you will feel empowered.

Here are some tips to help you.

- Consider what your fear is costing you each and every day. How is it holding you back and limiting the quality of your life? The cumulative effect of that is much greater than whatever you might fear. Can any short-term discomfort you experience from facing your childhood outweigh the daily limitations that fear may be causing you? I don't think so.

- Take a long, hard look at what is really frightening you. What do you expect to happen? What is the worst thing that can happen? If you consider these questions you'll see that failing to act in face of the fear is unnecessary. The things that can actually happen are probably a lot less devastating than you might think.

- Discuss your fears openly and honestly with a therapist or a friend with whom you feel comfortable. Knowing that you have the support of others can help you to move beyond your fears.

- Be willing to change. You may not know how to change yet, but just by being open and willing to change your energy will shift in new and positive directions.

- To change your thinking and support yourself use affirmations, such as, "I am willing to release the past and move beyond my fears," "I am open and receptive to change," and "I am now in the process of creating a wonderful new life for myself."

- Learn the Emotional Freedom Technique (EFT). This simple and gentle tapping technique is a wonderful tool to help release resistance and move beyond fear.

I began to address my childhood issues when I was in my teens and early twenties. Not only was I able to release many painful memories and experiences, but I made connections about the effects the past had on me. I gained valuable insight and understanding and was able to heal my emotional pain related to traumatic events. Initially, it was hard to open the door on the past, but I trusted myself enough to know that I could handle it. Ultimately, this freed me up in so many ways.

A heavy burden was lifted by examining my childhood and I was able to gain the presence of mind to more fully engage in my life. I hope that you find the courage within yourself to do the same. What are one or two things you could do over the next week to move beyond your fear?

GROWTH TIPS

It takes a lot of strength and courage to explore the past. Overcoming fear and moving beyond your comfort zone is the only way to make progress in any area of your life. Make a commitment to yourself by deciding to transcend your difficult childhood, finding positive resources and support, and then taking action to make the necessary changes.

CHAPTER EIGHT

Overcoming Adversity

*"Times of great calamity and confusion have
ever been productive of the greatest minds.
The purest ore is produced from the hottest furnace,
and the brightest thunderbolt is elicited from the
darkest storm."*
—Charles Caleb Colton

I've always been inspired by underdogs, people who have surmounted great odds to pursue their dreams, achieve success, and make a positive impact on the world. I'm not only talking about celebrities or the great leaders we know, those like Martin Luther King, Jr., Gandhi, or Mother Teresa; I'm talking about you. Yes, you. You struggled against adversity as a child and survived, and you need to be commended for it.

As someone who endured a difficult childhood, most likely you are still dealing with adverse effects. I believe you will surmount these, too. I know how hard it is to build a successful life when you have come from the trenches. I also know that it can be done. Like you, I've done it, and so have many others. The important thing to recognize is that you are not alone. Everyone experiences adversity at some point in his or her life.

People face all sorts of hardships: everything from physical and mental illnesses, to divorces and breakups, financial difficulties, natural disasters, the death of loved ones, bullying or harassment at school or at work, oppression, and homophobia, as well as abuse and neglect.

Adversity Can Come from External or Internal Sources

For the purpose of recovery, it's essential to recognize that adversity sometimes comes from outside forces and it also sometimes comes from within us. For example, if you were an abused or neglected child, the adversity came from the person who harmed you. If you are struggling with low-self-esteem and continue to berate yourself with negative thoughts and feelings today, the adversity is being generated from within.

External adversity is clear. There is an external force that pushes against us—for example, a threatening person, a social injustice, or a natural disaster—causing a negative impact upon our lives. The Great Depression of the 1930s and the economic crisis that began in 2008 are prime examples of external adversity. Growing up with an abusive parent is another example of an external adversity with which you have had to cope. It's important to understand that this type of adversity was caused by an outside source over which you had no control, so that you can stop blaming yourself.

Internal adversity is a bit more subtle than external adversity, making it harder to recognize. For example, a self-defeating attitude is a form of internal adversity that interferes with living our lives and being successful. Because it is generated from within, we are usually unaware of it. Internal adversity stems from negative programming: meaning, our core beliefs, attitudes, and paradigms.

A paradigm may be defined as a "set of assumptions, concepts, values, and practices that constitutes a way of viewing reality." Basically, it's a way of thinking and seeing the world that forms an inner program which you would act on, like an internal "operating system." You can therefore think of your inner programs as how you are "wired." Your mental and emotional "wiring" causes you to behave, act, and react in certain ways, some of which are positive and some of which are negative.

As a result of being raised in an adverse environment, you are likely to have internalized many negative messages about yourself and the world around you. As you came to believe these were true, you were being "programmed"—like a computer would be—by your environment. A belief is only a thought you keep thinking that ultimately becomes the truth for you. Fortunately, by practicing new thinking you can replace negative beliefs and inner programs.

Most likely, you are still being influenced by the beliefs of your parents, teachers, religious institutions, and others that were imposed upon you years ago. Some of these beliefs are positive and helpful, but many are detrimental to your current well-being. As adults, many of us are walking around with low self-esteem and a lack of confidence that has eroded our sense of self. Frequently, we are sabotaged by our own internal adversity, which is working against us.

Left unchecked, a negative operating system can inhibit our lives and keep us from living more fully in the present moment. This becomes a vicious cycle that we often find ourselves in, a thought loop, so to speak. If we become imprisoned by thought patterns, belief systems, or paradigms, like computers we need to reboot and upload new software into the operating systems of our minds.

To do this for yourself, start thinking critically about the beliefs and paradigms you operate within. Many of them are outdated and flawed premises that no longer serve you. You won't be able to make positive changes until you identify, address, and eliminate the thought processes that no longer work for you. You must therefore reprogram your mind with new beliefs that nurture and support you in the advancement of your goals.

Why make this effort? If I believed, *Everyone is out to get me*, how do you think I would function in the world? What about if I believed, *Everyone is always friendly and helpful to me?* Obviously, I would behave very differently and feel more ease with the second belief operating in my mind on a regular basis.

I recently discovered a longstanding belief of my own that I wanted to examine. The belief was, *Nothing good comes easy.* Have you heard that one before? Do you share it? When I took this belief apart, when I really tried to verify it, I found out that it wasn't always true. Yes, some good things in my life did not come easy to me and required a lot of hard work. However, many good things in my life did come easy. For instance, I have never struggled with my weight. That's something good that has come very easily to me. I have always had outstanding health, which is another example of something good that came easy to me. So the belief, *NOTHING good comes easy* is no longer true for me.

When you start to challenge your limiting beliefs and pick them apart, you will make similar discoveries. Our minds get so easily caught up in the negative that we tend to view everything in this way. That's why it's important to identify and examine our beliefs. It's the only way we can consciously change them.

What people choose to believe definitely makes a difference in how well they handle adversity in their lives. Therefore, take a moment to consider the following questions. Once you get clear on the source of the adversity you are facing, you can decide on the best way to address and overcome it.

How do you react to adversity?

What helps you to cope with it?

Can you recall a time in your life when you were able to overcome adversity? What was that like for you?

What beliefs are you still holding on to today? Are they serving you or harming you?

Post the following quote by Deepak Chopra somewhere where you can see it, as an excellent reminder to support you in transcending your outdated and flawed mental premises and paradigms.

> *"Every time you are tempted to react in the same old way, ask if you want to be a prisoner of the past or a pioneer of the future."*

Comparing Yourself with Others
Often Leads to Unhappiness

As human beings we have a natural tendency to compete and compare ourselves to one another. We usually do this to make a determination about how we measure up against our peers. As an adult who had a difficult childhood, it is common to ask, *Why me?* and fall into a trap of self-pity. We usually do this by using *upward comparisons,* meaning we never measure up to the person we are comparing ourselves to. This other person is always smarter, richer, happier, better looking, more successful, and has a nicer home, car, and whatever else than us—and *clearly* they didn't have to deal with all this childhood crap.

Upward comparison leads to the "keeping up with the Joneses" syndrome, a mentality in which people try to constantly match the lifestyles of their neighbors. It's a very dangerous road to travel in our thoughts because we rarely or never feel good enough in comparison to the people we admire. It's an unhealthy dynamic that can only lead to resentment, bitterness, and unhappiness.

If you catch yourself trapped in this negative thought pattern, there is a mental game you can play to counteract its effects. Instead of only doing upward comparisons, make a point to incorporate some *downward comparisons,* too, such as:

- How is your life better in comparison to some-

one less fortunate than you?
- What is good in your life that someone else would be grateful to have, too?
- What qualities do you possess that make you unique in the world?

This technique is not intended to be used to make you feel better than anyone else in an egotistical way, but rather to give you a more accurate self-appraisal of where you are in your life at the present time. The truth is that there will always be someone who has it better than you and someone who has it worse. Recognizing this truth will help you to become more grateful in your life.

Developing a Sense of Gratitude

While you may not be where you want to be in your life yet, it's important to remember that there is a process to everything you experience. You are on a journey and will continue to grow and evolve throughout your life. Thus, the number one quality you need to develop to enjoy the journey is patience.

Cultivating a sense of gratitude helps us to foster patience. Why? When you recognize the good that exists in your life, it keeps you grounded in the present.

You can be eager to accomplish your goals while still appreciating what you have and where you are in your life right now. Gratitude will immediately expand your energy and allow you to feel good. It will also help you to heal and transform your life much faster than you would otherwise.

Use the following exercise to practice being grateful.

Gratitude Exercise

Find a quiet place where you can take a few minutes to relax. Once there, close your eyes and take a few deep breaths. As you exhale, allow yourself to relax and become centered in your body and mind. Keep breathing deeply.

Take a few moments to think about all the things you are grateful for in your life. These can be very simple things, such as the fact that your heart is beating and you are alive. You might also be grateful for a specific person or relationship in your life. Think of whatever is meaningful to you.

One of the simple things that I am always grateful for is that I have a comfortable bed to sleep in at night. When I think about all the people who are homeless or living in shelters, I often think, *Thank you . . . thank you for this wonderful bed,* as I snuggle into it and go to sleep.

When you have identified some of the things you are grateful for, write them down in a gratitude journal. As you compose your list, really connect with each item you've identified and allow yourself to feel a sense of gratitude for it. You can add to your gratitude journal each day as you think of more and more people and things for which you are grateful.

It's wonderful to keep your gratitude journal on your nightstand so that you can review your different entries before going to sleep. This is a much better way to end the day than watching horror stories on the nightly news.

The Power of Resiliency

Resiliency is another important attribute of people who are able to overcome adversity. The ability to bounce back after a negative experience gives them optimism, hope for the future. Therefore, if you can positively respond, adapt, or cope after experiencing unhappiness or trauma during childhood it will make a huge difference for you. If you can be flexible and allow yourself to go with the flow, you will be able to successfully weather life's ups and downs. In many ways a resilient person comes back more powerful and stronger than before. They are able to take life's lessons and integrate them into their experience with increased knowledge and wisdom.

Resiliency enables you to take your power back. It allows you to take control of yourself and the choices you make; thus it will ultimately contribute to your overall success in life.

GROWTH TIPS

Identify the source of any adversity that is troubling you. Is it coming from external or internal sources, or both? Recognize that everyone faces adversity at some point in their lives. Incorporate downward comparisons to appreciate who you are, and where you are in your life right now. Cope with adversity by creating a plan to overcome it and developing a sense of gratitude and resiliency.

CHAPTER NINE

Inspiration

"People are like stained-glass windows.
They sparkle and shine when the sun is out,
but when the darkness sets in, their true beauty
is revealed only if there is a light from within."
—Elisabeth Kübler-Ross

C hildren naturally look up to the people around them as role models. Generally, their most important role models are their parents or caregivers. For children who have been the victims of abuse or neglect these role models are quite distorted. We now know the negative impact this can have on a person's life in adulthood. While others in the same situation are not so lucky, some children in troubled households are fortunate to have a least one parent who is a positive influence. As I stated earlier, I was extremely blessed to have an incredible, loving, and strong mother who was always a positive influence, and this made a big difference in my life—for this I am grateful.

It only takes one damaging parent to create a harmful and oppressive environment. This parent's behavior throws the entire family out of whack as all the attention is focused on dealing with cleaning up his or her mess. As a young boy, in my family, for instance, my father was both a negative role model and a non-existent figure. His presence instilled fear and anxiety while his absence created a void. Nothing my mother did could override his negative influence upon our family's existence until he was gone—and after he was gone.

Due to his alcoholism, my father was never available when I needed or wanted him. He never attended any of my school plays or events, and I was the only kid in Cub Scouts whose dad never attended a meeting or a camping trip. The pain of his absence intensified when I saw other kids interacting with their fathers, while wondering, *Where is my dad?* Instinctively, I tried to look up to some of my friends' fathers; unfortunately that didn't work out too well, as many of them were avoidant and cold. For some reason, many men of that generation were angry and distant, which always intimidated me.

My father never expressed an interest in my life or an ounce of concern for my well-being even after my parents divorced. He never provided any financial support. There was no college tuition, no pocket money, no car, nor any other "normal" gifts of things that a father would naturally be concerned about providing for his children. The lack of parental guidance from my father also left many gaps and unanswered questions, causing me to seek out answers, positive role models, and inspiration from sources outside of my immediate family. My mother did her best, but boys need male role models to teach them how to be men.

Sometimes life can be tough with seemingly no rhyme or reason. We may not always know why things happen the way they do, yet we are still left to pick up the shattered pieces and attempt to make order out of chaos. Oftentimes this causes us to expect less from life than we could so that we can avoid disappointment. We learn to, and then choose to tolerate life the "way it is," and can develop a sense of helplessness as a result. We may throw our hands up in the air, feeling, *Nothing I do makes a difference anyway, so why bother?* This sense of helplessness holds us back, leading to a state of inertia. Going down this road makes us depressed and causes us to live ineffective and unfulfilled lives—to which I say: Screw that!

You deserve so much more.

Create the Choice to Change Through Inspiration

In order to connect with your personal power, it's important to seek out positive role models, mentors, and sources
of inspiration. That's why I wrote this book. My number
one intention is to inspire and empower you to reach
for more in your life, more perhaps than you have ever
thought or dreamed was possible. Perhaps you do not
have someone to look up to in your life at the moment.
That's okay. The best way to get yourself out of a funk is
to start identifying sources of inspiration. You can do this
right now, from where you are today.

I'm going to ask you a few of questions that I want you to
really think about:

- Who inspires you?
- What inspires you?
- What makes you come fully alive?
- What makes you happy and joyful?
- Who do you like to be around?
- Why do you like to be around them?
- What qualities do they exhibit that
  you appreciate?
- What would it be like if you possessed these
  qualities, too?

Perhaps you enjoy playing sports, listening to or playing
music, going to the theatre, or watching movies. Maybe
reading and writing is a source of inspiration to you. These

are activities you can engage in on a daily basis. Start doing things that make you feel good. You can use these activities as a springboard to connect to people who inspire you. Initially, it might be a sports figure, celebrity, or hero that you admire from a distance, someone you identify with who allows you to believe in yourself and makes you feel that anything is possible. Let this role model inspire and motivate you to tap in to your own greatness.

Eventually, you will find people in your everyday life who are positive role models, mentors, and sources of inspiration and support to you, people you can interact with in person. You may need to draw on the strength of these people as you develop yourself and increase your self-esteem. Once your confidence increases, you will start to trust yourself more. You will then become an inspiration to others who may need to rely on you at some point in time.

Listening to my favorite singers during some of the darkest periods of my adolescence inspired me to want more from life. I used to put on the headphones in my room to drown out all the fighting and screaming that was going on around me. Music made me feel that anything was possible. As my desire for a better life expanded, I began to reach out to the people around me and developed relationships with teachers, directors, mentors, friends, therapists, and coaches who inspired me on my path.

Today, many people continue to inspire me every day.

People like my mother, brother, and sister, who were also able to overcome their difficult pasts to live positive, productive, and fulfilling lives. I'm also inspired by several of my friends, relatives, and clients who have had to overcome numerous adversities in their lives. A few of them have generously agreed to let me share their inspirational stories with you. Please note that the names were changed to respect their privacy.

Grace

Grace had a terrible childhood. She was born to unwed teenage parents who didn't want her and hoped to send her away. Grace was left to be raised by her paternal grandmother with whom her father still lived at the time. Although they were not her primary caregivers, Grace was nonetheless involved with her parents, who were verbally, emotionally, and physically abusive to her throughout the years. Grace's parents eventually married and had other children, but they always treated Grace as an outcast. Whenever Grace came to visit her brother and sisters, she was introduced to them as "some girl who lived in the neighborhood." Her siblings had no idea that Grace was their sister until many years later.

Grace told me, "One of my earliest memories was hearing my father and his mother fighting over me. I was only four-years old at the time. The yelling seemed to go on forever. They were deciding about what to do with me—deciding my fate. My father wanted me gone. He screamed that my mother had left me because she didn't want me, and he didn't want me either. My grandmother yelled back that she was worried about what people would think of them if they put me in an institution. My father said that he wanted no part of me and that if I remained in the home, I was to become my grandmother's responsibility. I remember thinking that it was the comment that 'people would think poorly of them' that saved me."

Grace transcended her difficult childhood, got married, and had a child of her own. She became a loving, nurturing, and compassionate person who worked for years in the field of social services, counseling and inspiring others to improve their lives. At the age of thirty-four, Grace's husband suddenly died from an illness. Now widowed, she was left to raise her seven-year old daughter as a single parent. Grace struggled for years to overcome the adversities in her life.

Today, Grace is a loving grandmother of two beloved grandchildren and she is actively involved in their lives. Although Grace was able to overcome her painful childhood, her mother was never able to move beyond her limitations in their relationship despite the attempts Grace made to grow closer over the years.

Grace told me, "More than five decades later, I was on one of my daily calls to my mother. She was fighting cancer and since distance and circumstances limited my visits,

I called. My sisters felt that my calls eased their burden. It was in the middle of one of these calls that my mother said, 'You have no family.' It hurt, but not in the way my four-year old self was hurt. I thank God for the blessing of my strength and all of the work I have done on myself to rise above my past."

What inspires me about Grace is her ability to so freely and willingly give to others that which she never received herself. When I asked her how she was able to do this she replied, "I didn't want other people to feel the way I felt. I also knew that I could do it. I saw how people responded to my kindness and the difference it made in their lives. If I couldn't take away my own pain, at least I could take away someone else's. I used to rescue animals, too." Her childhood experiences caused Grace to develop tremendous compassion for others, which she demonstrates in ways that have a positive impact on the world around her.

I'm fascinated by people who choose to change their circumstances, break the cycle of abuse, and move beyond a difficult past.

Jim

Jim was born and raised in a small Roma village in Romania. He never knew his father, as he left when Jim was a very small child. Jim was raised by his mother and maternal grandparents. He had a very difficult childhood, as the family struggled through immense poverty that they experienced due to the shortages imposed by Communism. Jim told me, "We had no electricity in my village. We had to wait on long, long lines for hours just to buy milk, meat, and chicken. It was terrible. Everything was rationed by the communist dictatorship. They used to give us a quarter of a pat of butter to last for a month."

Jim's grandfather had a lot of anger and he was physically abusive to Jim's grandmother and aunt. When he was eight-years old Jim tried to intervene to protect them, but his grandfather merely pushed him away and told him to shut up. As a young boy, Jim worked hard with his grandparents on the farm. He milked cows, fed chickens, and picked berries that he sold with his grandmother in the town. In September 1989, two months before his nineteenth birthday, Jim entered the Romanian army. In December that year, the people revolted against the dictator Nicolae Ceausescu. Initially, for the first week the army was on the side of the dictator, but then it turned against him and his secret service, the Securitate. Jim fought with the Romanian army who engaged in widespread fraternization with the opposition forces to overthrow the communist regime of Ceausescu.

In 1995, Jim won the DV1 Visa Lottery, which allowed him to legally come to the United States. He settled in New York City. Jim arrived alone and with no contacts. He was unable to speak or read English, and only had $600 dollars in his pocket. "I had no friends or family to turn to when I arrived in the United States. It was very lonely, but I was determined to live a better life than I had in Romania. Failure was not an option."

Jim located a Romanian woman who had an available room for rent in Queens. His first job was in a Romanian restaurant earning $10 dollars a day plus tips as a busboy. On most days he earned a measly $15 to $20 dollars for an entire shift. Later on, Jim worked other odd jobs to support himself, while he learned and studied English at Hunter College. In 1998, only three years later, Jim applied to, and was accepted by New York University, where he obtained a bachelor's degree in history and education. He became a United States citizen in 2002.

Jim graduated from NYU with honors and then continued to pursue higher education. He was accepted into NYU's master's program for politics and international relations. Today, he works as a special education teacher in New York City. He was able to purchase a home and has realized his dream of a better life. Recently, Jim was accepted into the doctoral program in history at Columbia University.

Sean

My cousin Sean and I have been through a lot together. We are only nine months apart in age and have been close since we were children. When my family relocated to

Queens after we lost our home and my parents divorced, Sean became my only true friend and companion. Sean lived a few miles away, and although I wasn't able to hang out with him every day we spent a lot of time together. We were both relatively isolated kids and so we relied on one another for support. Sean came from a large family and he was one of five children. His dad also had a drinking problem. A very stoic Irish man, Sean's father would frequently isolate himself from the rest of his family. He drank a lot of beer while watching television alone in the basement of their home.

During the 1970s, there was a lot of anti-gay rhetoric being spewed about. Specifically, Anita Bryant was spearheading anti-gay activism in Florida. She led a campaign to repeal an ordinance that prohibited discrimination on the basis of sexual orientation, and it was all over the news. Bryant perpetuated the fear that gay people would try to recruit and molest children, stating: "What these people really want, hidden behind obscure legal phrases, is the legal right to propose to our children that theirs is an acceptable alternate way of life. . . . I will lead such a crusade to stop it as this country has not seen before." There was also a lot of discussion about whether or not gay teachers should be allowed to work in the school system.

At the age of twelve, during junior high school, Sean began to struggle with depression. This was mostly triggered by bullying and harassment he received at school.

Sean and I attended different schools. I was in public school, and Sean attended a private Catholic school so we were unable to lean on one another during these incidents. One day, when we were both around the age of fifteen, I was with Sean at his house. He was visibly upset and shaken and asked to talk to me in private. We snuck downstairs to the basement boiler room and closed the door behind us. Sean was afraid to have anyone overhear what he had to say to me. Sean began to cry and he came out to me, saying, "Do you know what Anita Bryant is protesting against? Well, that's what I am."

I did my best to console and support him as much as I could at the time. He didn't know it, but I was also scared and uncertain about my own sexuality. I was definitely not ready to admit that I might have had similar feelings, and so I kept that to myself. As I said earlier, I was dealing with too much other garbage in my life to even look at this part of myself. Basically, Sean and I kept this secret to ourselves.

Sean told me that he thought about suicide. He showed me pills that he kept hidden in his dresser drawer. I was basically in denial and didn't take this threat seriously. I never believed that he would ever act on these feelings, so it didn't occur to me that I should tell someone. I also didn't want to ruin his trust in me.

One evening, we were celebrating a birthday at a nearby relative's house. At one point, the adult topic of conversation centered on homosexuality and the whole Anita Bryant controversy. Many of the adults there, including Sean's parents were in support of gay teachers being banned from working in the school system. I instinctively knew this would upset Sean and I privately asked him how he felt. He told me that he was okay. The next day, however, I learned that Sean had been taken to the hospital in the middle of the night due to an overdose.

When I put two and two together, I felt horrible and guilty that I never said anything to Sean about my own sexuality. I also just couldn't believe the suicide attempt happened. The night before, after he took the pills, Sean had been wandering around incoherently in the hallway. He was ultimately found by his sister when he accidentally walked into her bedroom and awakened her.

Sean left a suicide note for his parents telling them to ask me why he did this. My uncle came to pick me up to take me to the hospital to visit Sean after they pumped his stomach. I was alone with my uncle on the car ride to the hospital that day. The drive seemed endless as he asked me to tell him why Sean attempted to take his life. I was conflicted and extremely uncomfortable, but I nonetheless reluctantly told my uncle that his son was gay. He was stunned, and didn't know what to say.

Today, Sean and I remain very close. He struggled with depression for many years but was finally able to overcome it. Despite the adversities he faced as a child, Sean became a true success story. Initially, he had a successful career as an architect but he later decided to change careers. While working in the field of architecture, Sean began to do volunteer work with an HIV/AIDS organization. He was so inspired by the work he was doing to help others that he decided to go back to medical school to become a doctor while he was in his mid-thirties. Sean is now a successful medical doctor and does a lot of work with HIV/AIDS and cancer research. After working for years as a doctor, he then went back to school again and obtained a master's degree in public health.

Recently, I asked Sean what motivated him to pursue such a high level of education. He stated: "Putting all my focus into education was a sort of distraction for me. It took me outside of myself and helped me to successfully deal with depression." Sean has discussed his lifelong struggle with depression with me on many occasions throughout the years. Most recently those discussions have focused on the success of his treatment for depression, which he attributes to both psychotherapy and medication.

Endless Possibilities Await You

I am hopeful that these three real life stories inspire you and also help you to see that anything is truly possible if you put your mind to it. Let this be a defining moment for you. Make a commitment to turn your life around. You are the only one who can make a choice to do this.

What is it that you really want to achieve? Go after it.

What are the unshattered dreams that are still alive within you? Once you have identified them, dare to live them.

Spirituality and Inspiration

One of the primary sources of inspiration for most people is the belief in a power much greater than themselves. Many people rely on their faith to give them hope, strength, and courage during harrowing times. Having a sense of spirituality can empower you to move beyond your difficult childhood.

This doesn't mean that you need to practice any particular set of beliefs. Spirituality means different things to different people. Some people have a very strong connection to their faith and religion. They attend weekly services and practice and participate in specific rituals as a part of a larger congregation. For others, spirituality is more of a private personal matter. They may practice prayer and meditation, or commune with nature while taking time to reflect alone. Others connect to their spirituality through metaphysical practices and beliefs, utilizing universal principals to recognize that they are a part of something greater than themselves. There is no right way for everyone, so it's important to find the path that works best for you.

Two questions for you to consider are:

- What helps you cope during difficult times?
- What aspects of your spiritual practices do you find most beneficial?

Spirituality allows you to connect to your inner being, the larger part of you. It helps you to gain new insights, perspectives, and meaning from your life experiences as you place them into a larger context. In the long run, spirituality is really about going beyond yourself so that you can offer your personal contribution to the world.

GROWTH TIPS

Identify sources of inspiration through activities that allow you to feel good. Expand your horizons to develop relationships with people who can be positive role models and mentors to you, people who can inspire and motivate you to connect to your own greatness. Identify others who have transcended their difficult childhoods—and remember, if they did it, so can you. Tap into spirituality to join with the larger part of you. This will help you transcend the past and offer a personal contribution to others.

Lighten up

"A person without a sense of humor is like a wagon without springs. It's jolted by every pebble on the road."
—Henry Ward Beecher

We are all born with a natural sense of joy and playfulness that is our birthright. For most us though, this sense of fun tends to diminish as we become adults. One of the reasons may be that many people believe that they have to be serious in order to be taken seriously. But this is far from the truth. This idea was most likely imposed upon them by their parents and the educational system.

As children, many of us are taught to work hard, be regimented, and fit in with everyone else in order to compete and be successful in the game of life. The mantra we learn is: Go to school, work hard, and get a good education so that you can get a decent and secure job. Unfortunately, the game has changed, and this way of thinking is not too relevant in today's world. This outdated approach to living and working only breeds inhibitions and defensiveness, while stifling creativity and spontaneity, as it is counterintuitive to our natural state of being.

Developing a healthy sense of humor will serve you well in your recovery from the aftereffects of a difficult childhood, and throughout your entire life. Humor is a valuable asset. Humor helps you to realize that nothing is insurmountable and that you can handle whatever comes your way. The ability to lighten up doesn't mean that you aren't a serious person; it only means you don't take yourself too seriously. Laughter eases the burdens of life and lightens the load.

Have you ever laughed so hard that you started to cry? Have you ever laughed with someone at something so utterly ridiculous that you kept laughing at all the laughter? If not, you are missing out on one of life's greatest pleasures. Laughter brings joy that is contagious. Humor is an effective tool that brings people together and enhances relationships. Make people laugh and they will always want you around. The ability to find humor and laugh at yourself and with others will definitely aid you in times of struggle or uncertainty.

The Healing Power of Laughter

Many scientists and researchers have explored the benefits of humor and laughter, and it turns out that laughter is truly one of the best medicines. In 1979, Norman Cousins, a journalist and the editor of *The New York Evening Post* and *The Saturday Review*, published the bestselling book *Anatomy of an Illness* (Bantam Books). In his book, Cousins discusses how he cured himself from illness with laughter.

The story was this. In 1964, Cousins returned home from a trip to Moscow, Russia, and began to experience symptoms of severe joint pain and fever. He was diagnosed with an illness that attacks the connective tissues of the body, given a poor prognosis, and told he had little chance of surviving. During his hospital stay, Cousins began to do research on the effects of stress and discovered that it is detrimental to the immune system. He also read about the effects of negative emotions on health and reasoned that if this was true, then positive emotions should have the opposite effect and improve health.

Cousins discharged himself from the hospital and checked into a hotel suite. He hired a nurse to read him funny stories and play Marx brothers films. He also doused himself with massive doses of vitamin C, believing that the supplement would also help him. In Cousins' words: "I made the joyous discovery that ten minutes of genuine belly laughter had an anesthetic effect and would give me at least two hours of pain-free sleep. When the painkilling effect of the laughter wore off, we would switch on the motion picture projector again and not infrequently, it would lead to another pain-free interval."

Within a very short period of time Cousins was taken off all of his painkillers and sleeping pills. He discovered that laughter relieved his pain, allowed him to sleep, and ultimately cured his illness.

Benefits of Lightening up

Clearly, a good sense of humor with lots of joy and laughter has many positive benefits including:

- Stress reduction. Laughter relieves tension, relaxes the body, and increases energy.
- Strengthening the immune system. Laughter increases blood flow and helps to release pain-relieving brain chemicals called "endorphins," thereby improving your overall sense of well-being.
- Eliminating negative emotions. It's hard to be depressed, anxious, or angry when you are laughing.
- Improving relationships. When you laugh and have a good time with someone it bonds you.

Overall, it is clear that the ability to have fun makes life much more enjoyable. It increases creativity, helps us to problem solve, and breathes new life into our relationships.

Exploring your past and finding effective ways of over-coming its residual effects is not an easy thing to do. As you embark on your healing pathway you will face many challenges. You are reviewing a lot of past hurts and struggles, a process that may stir up many emotions within you. Allowing more humor, laughter, and joy into your life will counter some of the effects of the past, while keeping you grounded in the present.

How You Can Lighten up

So how do you begin to develop a sense of humor and in-crease joy and laughter in your life? Here are some tips to get you started.

- Watch funny plays, movies, or television shows. Like Norman Cousins, you can immerse yourself in comedies to get some great belly laughs going.
- Go to a comedy club. Seeing live comedians will really get you laughing. You can also get a better sense of how to view life situations from a funni-er perspective.
- Give yourself prompts to lighten up. Keep fun reminders around your home or office, like a silly toy or computer screensaver. Place photos of you with family and friends having a good time on your desk or nightstand.
- Spend time with fun people. Enjoy the company of others who are playful and happy. Minimize or

eliminate toxic people from your life. The chronic complainers will only pull you into negativity and drain your joyful energy.

- Get a puppy or kitten. A new pet is a great way to bring some joy and playfulness into your life. Puppies or kittens love to play and have fun, and they can be great companions, too.
- Spend time with children. Children are deeply connected to their well-being. You can learn many things from watching children interact with others. You can also play games with them to reconnect with your own playfulness and creativity.
- Take up a fun new hobby or pastime. Activities like juggling, bowling with friends, learning a new instrument, or acting in community theatre can provide ample opportunities to have fun.
- Laugh at yourself. Catch yourself when you are taking life too seriously. How can you lighten up the situation? Share funny stories with others about embarrassing moments or silly things you've done.

Having a sense of humor was a big help to me as I went through my own process of recovery. I have always been gifted with a wacky sense of humor. I love to entertain and to bring joy and laughter into the lives of my family and friends. I've discovered that humor not only helps me to cope with life's ups and downs, it helps the people around me to cope with theirs, too.

The ability to laugh is one of life's greatest gifts. As you move through your recovery, find ways to inject some humor into each day. Stop dwelling on the negative aspects of your childhood and your life. View it from a different perspective and allow yourself to laugh at the absurdity of it all. As adults, my brother, sister, and I can still laugh at some of the crazy things my father did when he was drunk. We know that his behavior was completely off the wall, but we can still find some humor in it. The humor provides emotional distance from the experiences and offers a sense of gratitude when we reflect on how we were all able to transcend our difficult childhoods.

I encourage you to lighten up and allow more humor, joy, and laughter to radiate throughout your life.

GROWTH TIPS

Recognize the importance of bringing more humor, joy, and laughter into your life. Surround yourself with joyful people who don't take themselves or life too seriously. Find ways to have fun and bring more laughter and joy into your life. Lighten up and don't take yourself so seriously.

Part Two

Beyond Therapy and Recovery
Reaching New Heights

> *"I am not what happened to me.*
> *I am what I choose to become."*
> —Carl Jung

In Part One, we focused on the psychological challenges you need to address to overcome the pain of a difficult childhood. I led you through a therapeutic process of healing and recovery from the emotional ties that bind you to the past. My purpose was to help you gain sufficient emotional freedom so that you would be clear to live your best life now.

In Part Two, we will focus on how you can begin to create the life you truly want. This is not always an easy thing to do. Having had a difficult past, you are working at a disadvantage. You've probably never had someone show you the ropes. In many ways you've had to fly by the seat of your pants, and learned in the school of hard knocks.

You may therefore still have limitations in certain areas of your life or have aspects of your personality that you still feel you need to develop. This is a great time to do another self-assessment in order to determine the areas you want to improve.

It takes desire, determination, commitment, and persistence to be happy and successful. You have to really *want* a better life for yourself. It must be a strong, all-encompassing need that drives you forward. Without it, you will become complacent, never challenge yourself, accept limitations, and settle for a life of mediocrity. Because you are reading this book this choice obviously would not be of interest to you.

The two chapters in this section of the book are about personal growth and development. Here I will utilize some coaching principles to get you started. Now might be a good time, therefore, to discuss some of the basic distinctions between psychotherapy and coaching.

Most, but not all, models of psychotherapy examine the past. Psychotherapy explores past and present emotional pain and hurts with a focus on treatment, healing, and recovery. Coaching, on the other hand, is about getting you from where you are to where you want to be in any area of your life. It focuses on the present and the future so you can clarify your goals and realize your vision.

On a practical level, coaching is about setting and achieving goals. On a spiritual level, coaching leads to a more purposeful and successful life. The ultimate goal is for you to reach your full, untapped potential.

In a nutshell, psychotherapy is more of a helping profession whereas coaching is more of a serving profession. Coaching is not appropriate for those who are currently in crisis or in need of emotional healing or recovery. If you are still in a crisis, seek counseling from a psychotherapist. Then come back to the chapters here in this section, which encompass many of the elements of a coaching approach.

This is a very exciting time for you because in many ways your life has just begun. Now you finally get to choose to create the life you want. To the best of my ability, I always keep this feeling of newness alive within me, and I encourage you to do the same. If you experience life as if it's always beginning and unfolding, you will constantly have a fresh outlook. You will leave yourself open to endless possibilities for the magic that can happen in your life—and it will.

As you reflect on where you are right now and dream about where you want to be, I'd like for you to consider and ask yourself the following questions.

- Where do I want to go from here?
- What's possible for me?

- How can I overcome the obstacles that are in my way?
- What do I need to do to get what I want? What actions do I need to take?
- What aspects of myself do I need to develop or improve? For example: Do I need to become more outgoing? Do I need to be more assertive? Do I need to set greater limits with people and learn to say no?
- Who can support me in reaching my goals?

This is the time for you to accept personal responsibility. Perhaps you need to learn about basic finances and investing so that you can secure your future. Maybe you need to go back to school to get a better education or college degree so that you can work in a field that you love and enjoy. You might need to improve your relationships through participating in training programs, personal growth workshops, and coaching so that you can learn how to communicate effectively and have healthier relationships.

Attending to your personal health and well-being is another area in which you'll definitely want to practice your skills on an ongoing, daily basis. Ideally, however, the goal is to be happy and fulfilled in every area of your life. Please be patient and remember that you are on a journey of self-improvement and discovery. You can never be "done," because you will always be growing, evolving, and changing—as we all will be. So pace yourself, relax, and enjoy the ride that is your life.

My life has never taken a linear path. It has had a lot of twists and turns in it as I have tried to find my way. I worked extremely hard to discover my passions, educate myself, and accomplish my goals. In adolescence and early adulthood, I worked odd jobs in different industries to support myself. I did landscaping, exterminating, retail sales, and home improvements (including carpet and tile installation, painting, and wallpapering). I was a freight elevator operator, cleaned homes and offices, and later worked in the restaurant and catering business as a busboy, waiter, and manager. I did all of this while I went to college and performed in numerous collegiate and Off-Broadway theatrical productions, as I pursued my acting career. Ultimately, I decided to go back to school to obtain a graduate degree in clinical social work and subsequently trained as a life and business coach.

The field of personal development has been a constant passion of mine throughout my life, so I decided to pursue it professionally. It allows me to make a contribution and have a positive impact on people's lives and the world around me. Learning all of these skills and having varied work experiences made me into a sort of Renaissance man. I love to learn and enjoy doing many activities. I never limit myself by thinking I can't do something. I know that I can accomplish whatever I choose to put my mind to, and that is an incredible thing to own within myself. Maybe it took me longer to find my path than some other people, but that's life. It's not perfect and it's not fair.

Everyone is not treated equally. Some people may have to take out loans or work their way through school and then work full time, just scraping by from the moment they graduate. Others may receive inheritances or are handed a pile of cash, a house, and a car by their affluent parents or grandparents. Things are not distributed equally, so it's important to make the most of whatever you've got! You can either allow the difference between your situation in childhood and the situation of others to consume you with anger, jealousy, and bitterness, or you can accept it for what it was and move on.

Remember what we discussed in Chapter 8: Everyone has adversities in life, so don't look outside of yourself with upward comparisons and make yourself feel bad. Look within. You are whole, capable, competent, and complete. You have a warehouse full of talents and resources within you just waiting for you to tap into them. So let's get started putting those talents to work.

CHAPTER ELEVEN

Mastering Your Mindset

*"Progress is impossible without change,
and those who cannot change their minds
cannot change anything."*
—George Bernard Shaw

All actions begin as mere thoughts. When you set out to achieve goals, negative thinking will pretty much stop you in your tracks. If you engage in negative thinking you will end up losing your drive and focus, which you need in order to get anything done.

I realize that I touched on the importance of changing your beliefs in Chapter 8, but I want to go into it a bit deeper here because I know that creating the proper mindset is so critical to achieving your goals. When you change your overall mindset, you can change the way you view your future and what is possible for you—and then you will experience better results, greater satisfaction, and more rewarding accomplishments.

Whenever you want to accomplish something, you must begin with an idea. You start with a thought or concept that originates in your mind. You cannot create something unless you believe that it's possible. Your mindset includes your thoughts, emotions, and beliefs (all of which many people would consider to be metaphysical concepts because they are not tangible). You need the right mindset in place to support and guide you towards your goals and unshattered dreams.

The other aspect of creation includes the practical strategies, or specific things you need to do, to bring your desires to fruition. These are the more tangible items that you take action on, such as planning, goal setting, networking, and so on. Most people tend only to focus on the action side of the creation equation. They try to figure it all out and push forward in extreme action to get things done. They don't recognize or acknowledge the inner processes that can more easily support them in the achievement of their goals. But it's important to work on both aspects of creation, the mindset and the practical strategies, as you go after what you want.

My intention here is to support, inspire, and empower you to take your life to the next level in any area you are seeking to change. Perhaps you want to improve your health and well-being, lose weight, find love, increase your income, or start a business. Whatever you want to achieve, I encourage you to start from the inside by changing your mindset. You want your thoughts, beliefs, and emotions working for you, not against you. Who do you need to be to get what you want? Start being that person now. You can change who are being on the inside by eliminating the negative beliefs you have held that were impeding your progress. Doing this sets a solid foundation to build the future that you want.

Negative thoughts, beliefs, and emotions block creation.

As I've said earlier, we all have negative programming. If we had difficult childhoods, then most of what was put into our minds as children was negative. We adopted fears, doubts, superstitions, and negative thoughts and beliefs about ourselves, others, and the world around us. Most of this programming led us to the conclusion that we were not good enough and we didn't deserve to have the things we wanted in life. Many of these beliefs became a part of us over the years, and we didn't challenge them after a while. We may have been unaware of their impact, yet they frequently caused us to sabotage our efforts when we were striving for something better in our lives.

How many behavioral patterns do you continue to repeat over and over again even if they make no sense to you anymore? Have you thought about why you continue to do them? Have they merely become habits? Do you do them because that's what you were taught to do, and you never questioned what you were told? Which of these outdated habitual thoughts, beliefs, emotions, and behaviors that no longer serve you can you let go of now?

It's time to become a critical thinker. Start to evaluate the facts, opinions, and the sources of your behavioral patterns and beliefs in order to determine their validity. Ask yourself, *Is this really true for me? Maybe it was true or served me in the past, but is it still true and necessary today?*

Even if you are unaware of it, I want you to realize and accept that there is a dynamic internal process fully active in your life. The process at work is that your conscious or unconscious beliefs cause you to take or not take action, and that action or inaction leads you to the results that you have in your life. Your past beliefs and actions got you the results you have today. If you continue to operate in the same way now, you will get the same results in the future.

Now, if you like where you are and what you've created for yourself, then great, keep it going. If, however, things are not going well and you feel miserable, I have good news for you: You can always make positive changes to create the life you want. Start by examining your beliefs in all life areas.

- What do you believe about yourself?
- What do you believe about money?
- What do you believe about your health?
- What do you believe about relationships?

Begin to challenge and eliminate beliefs that are working against you. Additionally, identify the beliefs that are empowering you so that you can continue to enhance them throughout your life.

The following exercise will get you started.

Examining Your Beliefs

Grab a pen and a sheet of paper and make two columns at the top of the page. Above the left-hand column write the words "Empowering Beliefs." Above the right-hand column write the words "Limiting Beliefs." List your beliefs in both columns—the beliefs that support and empower you on the left, and the beliefs that limit you on the right.

Now examine your two lists. The areas of your life that are producing good results are likely areas where you have empowering beliefs about your abilities and what you can accomplish. You can view these beliefs as your *personal assets*.

You can probably also see some negative, limiting beliefs relating to the areas of life where you are not getting the results you want. These beliefs may be viewed as your *personal liabilities.* These are the beliefs that need to be challenged and ultimately changed. Go through the list of limiting beliefs or liabilities and eliminate each of these beliefs one by one by asking yourself the following questions.

- What price have I paid because of this belief?
- How is this belief affecting me financially, physically, and emotionally?
- What will happen if I continue to hold on to this belief?
- Where did this belief come from to begin with? Is it really true?

Then ask yourself:

- What would I have to believe in order to succeed in this area of my life?
- Who do I have to be to have what I want?
- What do I have to do differently in order to produce the results I want?
- What kind of empowering beliefs do I already have that I can apply to this area of my life? (You can review your empowering beliefs and use them to answer this question.)

It takes daily practice to cultivate a positive, healthy mindset. Our minds get so easily stuck on the negative. We get caught up in all the mind chatter that pulls us away from our joy and what we want to achieve. We become distracted and unfocused and then wonder why life doesn't work out for us. This is why it is so important to practice putting yourself into the proper mindset each day by developing a daily routine.

Just like exercise, you can't do it once and expect positive results. It is the same with working on your mindset.

Pay attention to what you think and say every day. Take part in activities that connect you to your well-being. Perhaps you would enjoy prayer, meditation, visualization, writing, or speaking positive affirmations, reviewing your gratitude list, or doing things that bring you pleasure. Experiment and discover what activities work best for helping you cultivate a positive mindset. The ultimate goal is to have your mindset—your thoughts, emotions, and beliefs—aligned with your actions.

Once you are no longer blocking or sabotaging your efforts you will be much more successful in reaching your goals. Remember your thoughts, beliefs, and emotions lead to actions, which lead to results!

GROWTH TIPS

Develop your mindset to ensure that your thoughts, beliefs, and emotions are in alignment with your actions. Negative thoughts beliefs and emotions block creation. Examine your beliefs to determine which ones empower you and which undermine your efforts. Just like working out, you need to practice improving your mindset and your overall state of well-being on a daily basis. Remember that thoughts, beliefs, and emotions lead to actions, which lead to results.

CHAPTER TWELVE

Purposeful Action

"If you limit your choices only to what seems
possible or reasonable, you disconnect yourself
from what you truly want, and all that is left
is a compromise."
—Robert Fritz

In the last chapter, we discussed the importance of identifying and eliminating negative beliefs from your life. Doing this clears the way for you to focus on your goals. The process of creation is always the same. You wouldn't paint a room without first scraping off the loose paint chips, repairing the cracks, and priming the walls. You wouldn't plant a garden without first pulling out the weeds, turning the dirt, and fertilizing the soil. It's the same thing with creating things that you want in your life. You need to do the prep work and set a solid foundation to support your actions.

Now that you have eliminated the negative blocks that can sabotage your success, it's time to identify what is truly important to you so that you can develop a powerful vision for your life. Once you have a clear vision, you can set strong intentions for what you want to create, and then take the necessary actions to achieve your goals. Doing this groundwork allows you to take actions that have meaning and purpose.

I realize that I'm pushing you to go deep on this stuff, but I'm doing it so that you can really create a foundation that is aligned with your true self. Many people put the cart before the horse. They set up goals for themselves and take impulsive actions on things that are misaligned with their best interests and desires. Once they achieve their goals, they often realize it wasn't what they really wanted in the first place. I want you to know what is of utmost importance to you.

What are some of your core values? What are the things you hold in highest regard? What makes your heart sing? These are the things that you need to stay focused on.

I'd like to share an excellent analogy with you about identifying and remaining focused on what is truly important in your life from the book *Monetize Your Passion* (iUniverse, 2010) by Rich German. He compares the way we typically run our lives to juggling balls. Basically, in our lives we are juggling many things: work, family, home, health, finances, and so on. We juggle so many balls, in fact, that it's hard to keep them all in the air at the same time. Instead of giving all of these balls equal importance, start thinking of them as rubber balls and crystal balls.

What happens if you drop a rubber ball? It's no big deal because it bounces, right? You can always catch a rubber ball. Well, what happens if you drop a crystal ball? It shatters into a thousand pieces and it is gone forever. Not good!

What are your crystal balls? What are the main things that are most important to you in your life? These might include your health, family, spouse, or significant other, and so on. Identify three to five crystal balls and then keep your primary focus upon them. Don't ever drop a crystal ball.

When you understand what is truly important and what you value the most in life, you can make decisions and create circumstances to support it. The more aligned you are with your values and the things that are important to you, the more satisfaction you will have in your life. This is how you get happy!

Creating a Strong Vision for Your Life

Now that you have a handle on what's important, you need to create a vision to support you. You may not be where you want to be in your life yet, but that's okay. You are where you are, and you can always grow and change. Your vision is the engine that drives you toward your goals. When things get rough, when you hit an obstacle or snag, your vision will keep you going. Creating a vision will give you the fuel to propel you to where you want to be.

Do you have a vision for your life? Most people tend to take life as it comes. They go through life willy-nilly without having put in place a strong vision, the map of a clear direction, or a sense of purpose. Think of your life as your personal work of art. You have a blank canvas in front of you and you get to choose what you want to create. So what do you want to paint on your canvas?

- What is the vision for your life?
- Why do you do what you do? What is driving it?
- What is your mission?
- How do you want your life to be going forward?
- How do you want to spend your time?

If you get stuck while developing a vision, think about some of your early hopes and dreams.

- What were you excited or passionate about as a child or adolescent?
- What drove you?
- Who did you admire?
- What tasks or activities made time stand still whenever you did them?

Reconnect with these things and explore them within yourself.

Ideal Day Exercise

Imagine your ideal day. Visualize what it would be like to live the life you want. Really get into the feeling and experience it.

- What would your ideal day be like?
- What time would you get up?
- What would you do?
- Whom would you interact with?

As you go through this exercise, let go of any negative thoughts or conditioning that come up, thoughts such as, *Oh, I can't do this, Who am I to think I can live like this? Why should I get to live like this when the rest of the world doesn't? I don't deserve to have this.* Let go of these thoughts for the moment and allow yourself to experience and enjoy the exercise.

Really connect to the feeling of joy that your ideal day gives you. How would it feel to have what you want? How would it feel to be tremendously successful? How would it feel to do what you love? How would it feel to have transcended your difficult childhood and be living a happy and successful life?

Setting Your Intention

Think about your number one goal right now. Then think about where you want to be in the next six months to a year. I want you to set intentions for it.

An intention may be defined as a "course of action that one tends to follow or an aim that guides an action."

Setting strong intentions empower our lives. You may have goals or dreams that you want to achieve, but if you don't set a clear and strong intention about them, those goals and dreams will lack focus. They will be so foggy in your mind that most likely you won't achieve them. You want to set clear strong intentions so that you have a definite target to aim for in your mind.

What do you want to create? When do you want to accomplish it by? An intention can be specifically related to a goal or action, or it can be about a quality or state of being. A specific action-oriented intention might be: "I intend to pay all my bills today" or "I intend to make a delicious chicken dinner tonight."

An intention related to a quality or state of being might be: "I intend to have fun today" or "I intend to remain calm and serene no matter what happens around me."

You can set intentions about the goals and dreams you want to achieve and about your personal states of well-being.

Here is a four-step process that will help you to set intentions:

- Get clear about something you want and write down an intention for it. When you put something in writing magic happens. You have to formulate your intention into words and take it out of your head for it to become something concrete. A written intention makes it real. It is best to write intentions with a pen and paper as the act of thinking, formulating words, and handwriting allows for a deeper connection to the intention within you.
- Share your intentions with someone who will support you and hold you accountable. This could be a friend, spouse, significant other, or a life coach. Do this with someone you trust. Don't share your intentions with people that are negative or judgmental, as their responses could raise doubt and fear within you and undermine your efforts.

- Do something each day to demonstrate your commitment to your intention. These can be small action steps that you can take each day.
- Acknowledge and celebrate each accomplishment and take the next logical step so that you are always moving toward your goal. Celebrate your wins and accomplishments!

Connect with Your Higher Self

To take your intentions even further, you can connect them to your higher self, the non-physical part of you that is linked to the universal energy where all creation begins.

In his book *The Power of Intention* (Hay House, 2004), Wayne W. Dyer, Ph.D., discusses the concept of merging your individual thoughts with the universal mind. "Our individual thoughts create a prototype in the universal mind of intention. You and your power of intention are not separate. So, when you form a thought within you that's commensurate with Spirit, you form a spiritual prototype that connects you to intention and sets into motion the manifestation of your desires. Whatever you wish to accomplish is an existing fact, already present in Spirit. Eliminate from your mind thoughts of conditions, limitations, or the possibility of it not manifesting. If left undisturbed in your mind and in the mind of intention simultaneously, it will germinate into reality in the physical world. . . . Know that your thought or prayer is already here. Remove all doubt so that you create a harmonious thought with universal mind or intention. When you know this beyond doubt, it will be realized in the future. This is the power of intention at work."

If you would like to explore these concepts further I highly recommend that you read Dr. Dyer's book.

This and the other preceding exercises will influence the actions you take. When you are presented with an opportunity you can decide if it resonates with your values, vision, and intentions. You can be sure that the actions you take with this type of decision making will not only get you closer to your goals much faster, but will also lead you to greater happiness and fulfillment in life.

GROWTH TIPS

Identify what is truly important to you and stay focused on the activities in your life that you most value—your crystal balls. Create a powerful vision for your life to support you in the achievement of your goals. Set strong intentions to be clear of what you are aiming for. Develop a solid foundation that supports your decision making so that you can take purposeful actions aligned with your values, vision, and intentions.

Epilogue

"The fact that I can plant a seed and it becomes a flower, share a bit of knowledge and it becomes another's, smile at someone and receive a smile in return, are to me continual spiritual exercises."
—Dr. Leo Buscaglia

I'm honored that you have chosen to spend time with me, reading this book. If your childhood was difficult, I realize that the concepts and stories presented here may have been hard for you to face. I have pushed and challenged you to grow in many ways. I know that not everyone could follow the path I've outlined here. Some of my readers may do nothing with the information I have provided—perhaps choosing a different road to recovery than I am recommending. Whatever road you choose for yourself, just know that the concepts and insights I've shared will certainly support you.

If you've implemented any of the strategies I've suggested, then I admire your strength and courage to overcome your difficult childhood and change your life. If you haven't yet done so, do not beat yourself up. You will when you are ready. Either way, I encourage you to stay connected to your unshattered dreams and desires for a better life. As you do, your desire for growth and expansion will give birth to new and exciting experiences. I promise you that you will find yourself interacting with people on a level you perhaps never thought was possible. As your life continues to improve, a greater meaning about it all will unfold before you.

I can recall what it was like working as an account executive for a management consulting firm on Wall Street. In this role, I often counseled, trained, and coached senior executives, attorneys, business leaders, and human resources professionals in the business community. There I was among remarkable people, all of whom were seeking my insight, guidance, and support. I also worked alongside many colleagues who came from privileged backgrounds. Some of them had gone to private schools and had enjoyed considerable emotional and financial support from their parents since childhood. None cared about my background. None cared about the struggles I had faced or the enormous odds I'd had to overcome in my life. It was irrelevant to us in our professional circumstances because now we were on a level playing field.

What frequently surprised me in the years when I worked on Wall Street was that I often embodied greater emotional maturity, integrity, and kindness than many of my colleagues. As I saw this, I came to realize that I was okay. In many ways my life was better for having gone through so much adversity. My childhood background, although tough, provided me with tremendous strength of character and a high level of resiliency and resourcefulness to meet life's challenges.

Although I was now on equal ground in the workforce, managing my life and remaining competitive in my career still wasn't easy, of course. Ours was a highly aggressive work environment and I demanded excellence of myself. My self-determination required me to stretch beyond my comfort zone in many ways and with great fortitude. No matter where I was, I wanted to be seen as a leader, never as a victim. Frequently, in quiet moments, I reflected on my childhood and what I had achieved since then. I knew that I could never have accomplished as much as I had without doing all the inner work I did on myself and without having received the support throughout the years.

Eventually, I came to realize that all people are basically the same. We are human beings with similar doubts, fears, and insecurities. Even people who come from healthy and supportive backgrounds grapple with these types of thoughts and feelings. Today, as a therapist and life coach, I hear them discussed all the time in my work. No one is immune. We all experience the same range of emotions, and this is what connects us to our humanity.

One of my intentions in writing this book has been to take the pain of what my family and I experienced and use it as a platform to empower and inspire you. I couldn't allow my horrible childhood experiences to have occurred for no reason at all. I had to imbue them with meaning, and wanted to offer a broader contribution in my work with others.

My hope for you is that you will embrace the knowledge and awareness you have gained from this book. Really use the information so you can begin to heal the emotional pain of your difficult childhood and ultimately take your life to higher and higher levels. The sky is truly the limit. Reach out and grab hold of those unshattered dreams that are still alive and yearning within you. I fervently want you to be happy and successful, and live the life that you so richly deserve.

I wrote the following song lyrics when I was seventeen years old. At the time, I was reaching for my own unshattered dreams. I composed the music and wrote the lyrics while I was in the midst of chaos. I share the words to my song, "Freedom," with you now in the hope that it inspires you to find freedom—whatever that word means to you—in your life!

Freedom

Rainbow clouds are in the skies.

Now is the time to close my eyes and dream.

Soaring high into the air with a feeling of strength and no despair,

Like a kite caught in the wind with a broken string, I'm flying free.

Then I swirl and I twirl like a clown.

On my face there is never a frown.

And I will be free to be me.

Freedom.

To fly with a dream.

To know that it's real when you're soaring through the air.

Freedom.

To shout it out loud.

To feel in your heart, the strength that keeps you going when you land.

Recommended Resources

Now that you have read the book, you may be considering the next steps on your journey. Mindful of the fact that you may want further information and resources, I have compiled a list of options for you. If you have already engaged in psychotherapy and resolved the issues from your difficult childhood, life coaching would be the next logical step to support you in reaching your goals.

Coaching and Consulting with Paul Novello

Paul Novello offers a variety of individual and group coaching programs, personal development products, and free resources. These are all available at:

www.paulnovello.com

www.lifesolutionsforgaymen.com

If you are just beginning your recovery or you are currently in counseling and seeking additional services, you can explore some of the behavioral health and recovery resources referenced below.

Counseling and Psychotherapy Services

There are a variety of ways that you can locate counseling and psychotherapy services. If you are interested in talk therapy, you will most likely search for a clinical social worker or psychologist. If you require an evaluation for possible medication you can seek the services of a psychiatrist. A psychiatrist is a medical doctor who is able to prescribe medication, such as an antidepressant. Some people may need to work with both a therapist and a psychiatrist.

You may have some questions, such as:

- How do I pay for these services?
- Will my insurance cover it?
- How do I get started?

If you have medical insurance that includes behavioral health services, call the 800 number on your benefits card and ask to speak to a representative in the behavioral health department. Once connected, ask the representative or clinician to review your outpatient mental health benefits. Find out if you have a co-payment and if there are any limits on the number of sessions you are entitled to per calendar year. Then ask for a list of in-network providers in your local area.

If you are an employee, find out if your employer provides an Employee Assistance Program (EAP) benefit. You can usually find the number on your company's intranet or within the benefits package information you were provided when you were initially hired. This is generally a free resource that provides short-term counseling, assessment, and referral services. An EAP counselor can assist you in accessing the appropriate resources for your particular situation.

If you are a high school or college student, locate the counseling center that is available to you at your school or university.

If you have no insurance coverage, don't despair; you can inquire about resources within your local community. Many individual providers and outpatient facilities offer rates on a sliding scale basis at a low cost. You can also inquire about free support groups that may be available to you as well.

You can also locate providers through the following resources.

The Therapy Directory at *Psychology Today*
The *Psychology Today* Therapy Directory lists clinical professionals, psychiatrists, and treatment centers that provide mental health services in the United States and internationally.
http://therapists.psychologytoday.com/rms/prof_search.php

Find-a-Therapist.com

Search through Find-a-Therapist's directory of verified therapists, psychologists, marriage and family counselors, social workers, licensed professional counselors, and psychiatrists.

http://www.find-a-therapist.com

1-800-LIFENET

A free confidential help line specifically for New York City residents that you can call twenty-four hours a day seven days a week. The hotline's staff of trained mental health professionals helps callers find mental health and substance abuse services.

http://www.nyc.gov/html/doh/html/cis/cis_lifenet.shtml

National Alliance on Mental Illness (NAMI)

NAMI is the nation's largest grassroots mental health organization dedicated to building better lives for the millions of Americans affected by mental illness. NAMI advocates for access to services, treatment, supports, and research, and is steadfast in its commitment to raising awareness and building a community of hope for all of those in need.

http://www.nami.org

Peer to Peer Counseling Services

In addition to working with professional counselors, there are other available resources that provide assistance, peer-to-peer counseling and support.

Adult Children of Alcoholics (ACOA)
World Service Organization
ACOA is a national organization. Through the website you can find a local chapter in your area.
http://www.adultchildren.org

Al-Anon Family Groups (Al-Anon)
Al-Anon is a national organization for the family members of alcoholics. Through the website you can find a local chapter in your area.
http://www.al-anon.alateen.org

GLBT National Help Center
The Gay Lesbian Bisexual and Transgender Help Center provides free and confidential telephone and internet peer-counseling, information and local resources for gay, lesbian, bisexual, transgender, and questioning callers throughout the United States.
GLBT National Hotline 1-888-843-4564
GLBT National Youth Hotline 1-800-246-7743
http://www.glnh.org

Recovery Resources

Here is a partial list of some of the national twelve-step programs that are available to you for recovery from a variety of chemical and behavioral addictions. Through their websites you can find a local chapter in your area, and information on meeting times.

Alcoholics Anonymous (AA)
http://www.aa.org

Narcotics Anonymous (NA)
http://www.na.org

Gamblers Anonymous (GA)
http://www.gamblersanonymous.org

Sexual Compulsives Anonymous (SCA)
http://www.sca-recovery.org

Overeaters Anonymous (OA)
http://www.oa.org

Shopaholics Anonymous (The Shulman Center)
http://www.shopaholicsanonymous.org

Crisis Intervention Resources

You may be in need of the following resources to help you with a variety of more urgent and emergency concerns as listed below. If you are unable to access these resources for any reason, please call 9-1-1 or go to your nearest emergency room.

United States National Suicide and Crisis Hotlines
http://suicidehotlines.com/national.html

National Hopeline Network:
1-800-SUICIDE (1-800-784-2433)

National Suicide Prevention Hotline:
1-800-273-TALK (1-800-273-8255)

National Child Abuse Hotline:
1-800-4-A-Child (1-800-422-4453)

National Center for Missing and Exploited Children:
1-800-THE-LOST (1-800-843-5678)

National Domestic Violence Hotline
The National Domestic Violence Hotline creates access by providing twenty-four hour support through advocacy, safety planning, resources, and hope to everyone affected by domestic violence
http://www.thehotline.org
1-800-799-SAFE (7233)

Gay Men's Domestic Violence Project
The Gay Men's Domestic Violence Project assists and supports victims and survivors of domestic violence, focusing on members of the GLBTQ community, to bring about responsive public policy, and to increase access to culturally competent services.
http://gmdvp.org
1-800-832-1901

Recommended Reading

James Allen, *As a Man Thinketh* (1902).

Richard Bach, *Illusions: The Adventures of a Reluctant Messiah*. New York, N.Y.: Dell, 1989.

Martha Baldwin, M.S.S.W., *Self-Sabotage: How to Stop It and Soar to Success*. New York, N.Y.: Warner Books, 1987.

Douglas Bloch, *Listening to Your Inner Voice: Discover the Truth within You and Let It Guide Your Way*. Minneapolis, MN.: CompCare Publishers, 1991.

John Bradshaw, *Healing the Shame the Binds You*. Deerfield Beach, FL.: Health Communications, 1988.

John Bradshaw, *Homecoming: Reclaiming and Healing Your Inner Child*. New York, N.Y.: Bantam, 1990.

Claude M. Bristol, *The Magic of Believing*. New York, N.Y.: Pocket, 1948.

Leo F. Buscaglia, Ph.D., *Living, Loving and Learning*. New York, N.Y.: Ballantine, 1982.

Rick Carson, *Taming Your Gremlin: A Surprisingly Simple Method for Getting Out of Your Own Way*. New York, N.Y.: HarperCollins Publishers, 2003.

Norman Cousins, *Anatomy of an Illness*. New York, N.Y.: Bantam Books, 1981.

Stephen R. Covey, *The Seven Habits of Highly Effective People: Powerful Lessons in Personal Change*. New York, N.Y.: Free Press, 2004.

Alan Downs, Ph.D., *The Velvet Rage: Overcoming the Pain of Growing up Gay in a Straight Man's World*. Boston, MA.: Da Capo Press, 2005.

Wayne W. Dyer, Ph.D., *The Power of Intention: Learning to Co-create Your World Your Way*. Carlsbad, CA.: Hay House, 2004.

Shakati Gawain, *Creative Visualization: Use the Power of Your Imagination to Create What You Want in Your Life*. Novato, CA.: New World Library, 2002.

Rich German, *Monetize Your Passion: Follow Your Heart and Create Life's Ultimate Win-Win-Win*. Bloomington, IN.: iUniverse, 2010.

Louise Hay, *You Can Heal Your Life*. Carlsbad, CA.: Hay House, 1984.

Susan Jeffers, Ph.D., *Feel the Fear and Do It Anyway*. New York, N.Y.: Fawcett, 1987.

Joe Kort, Ph.D., *10 Smart Things Gay Men Can Do to Improve Their Lives*. New York, N.Y.: Alyson, 2003.

Rokelle Lerner, *Daily Affirmations for Adult Children of Alcoholics*. Deerfield Beach, FL.: Health Communications, 1985.

W. Hugh Missildine, M.D., *Your Inner Child of the Past*. New York, N.Y.: Pocket Books, 1982.

Joseph Murphy, Ph.D., *The Power of Your Subconscious Mind* (1963). New Jersey: Important Books, 1963.

Antoine de Saint Exupéry, *The Little Prince* (1943). New York, N.Y.: Mariner Books, 2000.

Stanley Siegel and Ed Lowe, Jr., *Uncharted Lives: Understanding the Life Passages of Gay Men*. New York, N.Y.: Penguin, 1994.

Suzanne Somers, *Keeping Secrets*. New York, N.Y.: Warner Books, 1988.

Janet G. Woititz, *Adult Children of Alcoholics*. Deerfield Beach, FL.: Health Communications, 1983.

Acknowledgements

I want to thank my brilliant and fun editor, Stephanie Gunning, who helped me to make my unshattered dream into a reality. You are amazing!

My mother, brother, and sister who were there from the beginning: We are the only ones who will ever know what we endured and this has bonded us together for life. I love you.

I also want to acknowledge the many people who have been instrumental on my path, especially Alice Christy and Ken Wilson. Thank you to Marie and Joseph Molesso, two special people who gave me shelter from the storm. Thank you to the clients, friends, and relatives who graciously allowed me to share their stories; you are all truly gifted and remarkable people.

Finally, to my coach, Rich German, who gave me the inspiration and the energy to realize my vision. Thank you.

About the Author

Paul Novello, L.C.S.W., C.L.C., B.C.C., is an author, therapist and life coach in New York City. As a highly sought-after coach and consultant, Paul has worked with numerous organizations, including Fortune 500 financial firms, law firms, healthcare companies, small businesses, and non-profit organizations.

Paul has always been passionate about personal growth and development, and he loves to explore the possibilities. Paul works with all people regardless of gender or sexual orientation. He enjoys inspiring others to discover their true selves, reach for their goals and dreams, and create the lives they truly desire.

Recognizing and responding to a definite need, Paul created and developed Life Solutions for Gay Men, a personal development resource to empower gay men to achieve personal, professional, and financial success. He formerly produced and hosted a live radio talk show, "Gay Life Solutions." This was a featured show in New York City through Equality Pride Radio on AM 1600 WWRL.

Additionally, Paul has an extensive background in the performing arts and he has studied and applied various techniques throughout the years, including meditation, progressive relaxation, emotional freedom technique, and the Alexander technique.

You can locate Paul at: www.paulnovello.com and www.lifesolutionsforgaymen.com.

www.ingramcontent.com/pod-product-compliance
Lightning Source LLC
Chambersburg PA
CBHW072031080426
42733CB00010B/1853